The Music Inside

Inner Techniques to **Tap** into Your Potential,
Change your Beliefs and **Create** a Fulfilling Career

JENNY CLIFT

Copyright © 2016 Jenny Clift

All rights reserved. No part of this publication (including the free resources) may be reproduced, distributed, or transmitted in any form or by any means, including photocopying, recording, or other electronic or mechanical methods, without the prior written permission of the author, except in the case of brief quotations embodied in reviews and certain other non-commercial uses permitted by copyright law.

ISBN-10: 1523404744
ISBN-13: 978-1523404742

Testimonials

Here's what readers are saying about the book:

I'm reading your book again, this time Just for Me - and I can't begin to tell you how valuable it is! As well as reading...I've skipped ahead to the "making a blueprint" section, and am starting to fill in the "4 trimesters" (quarters) in order to get a full year's plan for my life, laid out in front of me.

I am SO grateful to have this system, I thank you from the bottom of my heart. One of the things that makes it easy (ish) is the examples you give from your own life.

Because we readers know you well, from having read through the previous chapters, the examples are truly crystal-clear. I've seen similar plans laid out in various Success programs and books, and the 'examples' have always been a bit confusing because they were just that: made-up examples. Yours are REAL. What a difference that makes.

— Elaine M. (Novelist).

I´ve read your book and I´m shocked at finding so many of my own thoughts.

— Leticia H. (Cellist).

Thank you so much for your book. I have read the first few chapters and I have very strong resonance indeed - on just about all counts, except my "violin" is my paintbrush and canvas. I did not paint for 5 years after a similar experience with an art professor, and it has been a long journey getting my spirit back.

After reading the first chapter, I was inspired yesterday and today to give myself permission to spend time on my artwork first, & then deal with the housework, and it has felt wonderful.

I am still holding the vision of somehow letting all of these paintings I have inside of me to come out. I do have the motivation of age as I will be 65 in January and know the time has to be soon or even better NOW!

Thank you again & looking forward to completing the rest of the book - and giving my paintbrush some action!

— Penny M. (Artist.)

I received your book yesterday morning, fully intending to read it after Christmas and all our company has left. But I couldn't resist reading the introduction to get a taste of what I had to look forward to reading...

I picked up your draft and read through your childhood years, and as you can tell in the act of picking it up again I was hooked. Last night I read in the middle of the night when insomnia struck.

I will write you an email after I've finished reading it, and I've marked places that I'll re-read before I write you as they have spoken to me, or defined something new or something that I've known, but in a new and concise way. (I loved your analogy of the goals and your holiday on a long boat in England.)

As someone who is a practitioner of EFT, Law of Attraction, meditation, and writing, "The Music Inside" is as important to me, who has fallen off my life's purpose wagon to some degree, as it is for those completely unfamiliar to very familiar with these methods, to get (or get back) onto our own life's purpose wagon so we may live a fulfilling life that honors and shares our own unique and genius gift.

— Berta B. (Lighthouse Coaching and Retreats.)

Are you in the 'wrong' job?

Do you feel stuck, fed up and unfulfilled?

You don't know how to move forward or who to turn to?

I've been there too!

This book is about my journey, in the field of music. It is about how I went from working at a job that wasn't right for me, and how, using inner techniques to make outer changes, I moved into the job that I love.

You will discover here the tools and techniques that can help you on your own journey.

Learn how to:

- Move into the life and career that you really love.
- Use EFT ('Emotional Freedom Technique' or 'Tapping') to change your beliefs about yourself and become successful.
- Meditate easily, quickly seeing benefits in your life.
- Use writing exercises to discover your 'passion' and feel great about your life and yourself.
- Make a 'blueprint' – set your goal and create a 1 Year Action Plan.
- Access outside support and inspiration

I've created a few resources to assist and inspire you as you go through the book. You can get free instant access to them by visiting the links listed throughout the book.

Free Bonuses!

As a thank you for buying my book, here are the first free bonuses to accompany your 'Music Inside' journey.

This bonus package includes:

- AUDIO VERSION OF THE WHOLE BOOK read by the author.

- 1 VIDEO: 'Introducing EFT' where I explain a little about Emotional Freedom Technique (which, as I write in the book, has helped me in changing my life and career) and show how a 'tapping round' works.

- 4 MP3 AUDIOS with music arranged and played by 'The Laurus Freestyle Duo', Jenny Clift, violin and Cy Williams, guitar:
  'The Flowers of Edinburgh' Trad. Scottish Reel.
  'Gymnopedie No.1' by Erik Satie.
  'Danny Boy' Trad. Irish Air.
  'Crossfire' by C.Williams.

> Visit the link below to get instant access.
>
> *www.jennyclift.com/freebonuses1*

Dedication

This book is dedicated to my husband Alfonso, and my daughters Elisa, Emma and Silvia, my greatest supporters and my 'here and now'.

And to my parents and to my sisters who started all of this.

And to Brad Yates, my EFT Life Coach, without whom this part of the journey would have been very different.

Table of Contents

Foreword

PART 1: The Set Up

    1.1 Introduction
    1.2 Background — Childhood
    1.3 — Trinity, non-violin years and the first attempt
    1.4 — Teaching years

PART 2: Tap to Change

    2.1 EFT — 'Keep calm and keep tapping'
    2.2 What's stopping you? — Limiting beliefs
    2.3 — Limiting beliefs to liberating beliefs
        #1 'I'm too old'
        #2 'I'm not good enough'
        #3 'I'm not talented enough'
        #4 'There aren't any jobs/opportunities out there'
        #5 'I can't afford it'/ 'I don't have time'
        #6 'I don't want to rock the boat'
        #7 'I can't earn a living doing what I love'
        #8 'I don't know how to do it'

		#9 'I'm not an Artist/ professional violinist'
		#10 'I don't deserve it'
		#11 'I can't handle change'
		#12 'I'll fail'
		#13 'I'll succeed'
2.4	Following your heart	– Opening up to possibility
2.5		– 'What are you here to do?'

PART 3: Building a skyscraper – More Tools

3.1	#1 Writing	– Gratitude exercises
3.2		– '70 x7'
3.3		– Keeping a daily log
3.4		– 'Intentioning'
3.5	#2 Meditation	– My meditation story
3.6		– Benefits of meditation
3.7		– Practical tips for meditation
3.8		– Five stage meditation

PART 4: Building a skyscraper – Plan and Act

4.1	The Blueprint	– Guidelines
4.2		– Making your blueprint
4.3		– Mindmapping
4.4		– One year plan
4.5		– Plan of action
4.6	Get Building	– Taking action
4.7		– The Chinese takeaway restaurant

PART 5: Don't do this alone

| **5.1** | Outside help | – Get inspired |

5.2	– The 'perfect' Life Coach
5.3	– I'd love to stay in touch!

To pick up all the free resources which you will find as you read through the book go here:

www.jennyclift.com/freebonuses

Acknowledgements

About the Author

The Music Inside

Foreword

by Brad Yates, C.Ht.

(Author of 'The Wizard's Wish'
- coauthor of 'Freedom at Your Fingertips.')

Since you have picked up this book, it is quite possible that you, like most people (if surveys are to be believed), are not entirely satisfied with your life... particularly when it comes to the work you do. And like many people, you may feel you just don't know what to do about it, and so it has seemed easier to just keep going along. Not because there's something wrong with you, but because that is how most of us are trained to do it.

Fortunately, you now have in your hands a fantastic guide that can help you find your way out - a way to create a life you really love.

For many, whether the work they do is enjoyable doesn't factor into the equation - it's all about the expected outcome. More often than not, that is about the money - whether it's an impressive income or just enough to put food on the table. But there are other results that drive people, including the perceived prestige of certain careers or maybe just to make someone else happy (often a parent). And there's nothing wrong with any of that... but there is a more enjoyable way, and you deserve that. That fact that you are reading this book might suggest that you already know that.

I'm one of those fortunate people who actually loves the work I do. I greatly enjoy the process - right there in the moment. All the wonderful outcomes are icing on the cake. Including the opportunity to see my clients flourish, as Jenny Clift is doing. It's an immense pleasure to celebrate with her as she achieves goals that she had once doubted were possible.

I've often told clients and audiences, "I don't really do this work for you... I do it for all the people that you are going to touch in a positive way as you allow yourself to be free from what stops you." It is very rewarding to see that not only has our work together allowed Jenny to share her music with more people, but that she is also now sharing her journey in this book, which will help you share yourself in a more joyful way with the world. Because even though many of these tools and suggestions have been offered before, Jenny's unique way of sharing them is going to be the best way for many people to receive them.

Just as you doing what you love - sharing the music that is uniquely inside you - is going to be a gift to others.

Thank you for being willing to do that.

Be Magnificent!

— *Brad Yates*

Part 1
The Set Up

1.1 Introduction

"Most people die with their music still locked up inside them."
— Benjamin Disraeli

'Oh my God. I've got to get out of here or I'm going to end up killing one of these four year olds...'

Picture me, violin in hand, a classically trained musician, sitting on the floor in the corridor of a private English school, surrounded by four little kids who were half lying, half sitting, and half paying attention.

I was coming up to my 50th birthday...

I was making great money. I'd built up my teaching practice from only two to sixty students over twelve years. I was with the violin all day. I was my own boss....and yet...I was miserable and fed up.

Bored, frustrated and totally stuck. I knew there was something very wrong here but I didn't have a clue how to change things.

Maybe you can relate. Are you too in the wrong job?

Are you working at something, which, in your heart of hearts, you know is not what you came here to do?

It may be a rubbish job or it may even be a great job…but you know it's not *your* job. Maybe you just slid into it to satisfy someone else's idea of what you 'should' do. Maybe it felt right for you once or maybe it's all you feel you deserve or that you aren't good enough to do anything more rewarding.

Whatever the reason, you don't feel good. You feel unfulfilled, unsatisfied, fed up, and downright angry. The time is ticking and yet you don't know how to make a move, what steps to take, or even if you really should do this. After all, don't most people work at a job they don't really like…?

And who am I to 'follow my bliss'?

That moment sitting on the floor at school was a smack upside the head for me. I remember thinking, *'I'm going to be here for another fifteen years, then I'll retire, and I won't have done what I really want to do in this life.'*

I knew what I had always *wanted* to do.

I wanted to be performing; practicing, rehearsing and playing. Up there on stage sharing the music that I could feel so strongly inside myself.

At the weekends I was concertmaster (first violinist) of a semi-professional (I couldn't bring myself to say amateur) orchestra; and with them I was playing a concert each month in Madrid's National Auditorium. I was performing beautiful classical repertoire that speaks to me so much, and I was even invited to play solos with the orchestra from time to time.

For me, absolute bliss was a three hour rehearsal on a Sunday morning, two hours practicing at midday (my husband kindly looking after our three daughters back at home) and another three hours of rehearsal in the afternoon. I didn't get tired, I didn't see it as work, I didn't care that it was Sunday. I loved every moment of it.

After all, I was doing what inspired, energized and fascinated me.

So, yes, I did know what I wanted to do, **but I didn't know how to turn that passion into a living**. It felt impossible and I had a laundry list of reasons why I couldn't be a professional violinist –

I'm too old,
I'm not good enough,
I started too late,
It's just not 'me',
How can I rock the boat?
I don't have anyone to help me,
How can I walk away from a perfectly good job with the economic situation the way it is now?

I really didn't see that it was possible for me at this stage, but at the same time, that life was eating me up from the inside. Looking back I realize that's exactly what had to happen – I needed a change from the inside out.

And so I *did* make it happen. **Not overnight.** But I started the process that has led me to where I am now – a new place of possibility and job satisfaction. A place where I know that I am doing the right thing at last.

Along the way I have met many new people and have made friends and found mentors who have supported, guided, and taught me many things throughout my journey. I have even improved the relationships I already had, as I have become a happier, more confident, and fulfilled person.

I wrote this book to share my experience with you and to show you that it *is* possible to identify the work and lifestyle you want to have. It *is* possible to make that move. It *is* possible

to feel happy and content with a sense of purpose more than just on your days off.

Like me, you'll be starting from the inside out, working on your inner self in order to make the outer changes happen and really stick. This book will give you practical steps and advice to make this process doable, and yes, deeply satisfying, nurturing and enjoyable.

I went from being a full time violin teacher, doing a bit of performing on the side, but so frantically busy that I barely had time to practice. Now, four short years later, I am a professional freelance player, working and making money doing what I love – and, best of all, feeling great as I do it!

I am confident and know for certain that this career will expand and grow as *I* expand and grow as a person.

By following the steps I took, and by using the tools and techniques that I describe in this book - chiefly EFT (Emotional Freedom Technique), meditation and writing exercises - and by going at it from the inside out, the 'music' inside you, whether it be literal music or your own vocation, is attainable, and you *will* come to place of being much happier and satisfied with your life. This is the start of a new journey, but this time with the certainty that you are on the right path.

I now have two CDs out there with my violin and guitar duo and we play paid concerts in Spain, England and the US regularly. I have videos on Youtube. I belong to and make recordings for Paul Santisi's MusicMastermind group. I've published two online video courses teaching violin to adults (paid $1,000 up front) and have just signed a contract to play with a professional symphony orchestra here in my home town for the 2015/16 season.

I know from my experience that it can be done, that it is possible, and in this book I provide you with the steps that I took to make all of this happen.

I promise that by taking this journey you will change the way you feel about yourself, become the kind of person you want to be, and from there, start taking the actions you need in order to change your life, your career and become a much happier, more successful and satisfied person.

You will come to know deep inside that you are on the right track, doing what you are really meant to be doing.

It took me FIFTY YEARS to get to this point!!

Don't be, like I was, the kind of person who keeps putting it off, resigning themselves to the status quo, making the best of a bad job, and slowly dying inside.

Start now, wherever you are, however old you are, and be the kind of person who makes a fulfilling life for themselves. Become the kind of person who jumps out of bed in the mornings excited about what the day ahead holds.

This is the story of how I decided 'what I wanted to be when I grew up', how I ran away from it for nearly a decade, rediscovered my 'calling', almost made it but then settled for second best. It is the journey I took to learn what I needed to know and be able to move into what I love.

Take control of your own life right now. No one should die with their music still locked up inside.

1.2 Background - *Childhood*

So how exactly did I get to that place on the floor?

Why wasn't I a successful, performing violinist, sharing my gifts and my music with millions?

Well, the short answer is 'fear'.

And as for the long answer…

I reckon you could say that my early childhood was pretty idyllic.

I was born right after my twin sister, in Versailles, France, where my father, a British Diplomat, was posted at the time. My arrival was unexpected. 'Il ya une autre' ('There's another!') cried the French midwife as I appeared. My parents took it on the chin, quickly thought of a second girl's name, and so my life began.

Pam, my twin, and I were inseparable. A unit, often ganging up on our older sister, Lucy, but also obediently following her directions to 'be horses' or play all sorts of games. We moved to England when I was 18 months old, then a few years later, to Malaysia, China (at the time still under the communist regime and Chairman Mao), Northern Ireland (with all the political 'troubles') and then Canada.

We soaked up sights, sounds, smells and experiences along the way, living in these exotic, foreign countries, partaking of their beauty and strangeness and yet not really one with them. We ate breakfast on the Great Wall of China, played among the ruins of the Ming Tombs, frolicked on idyllic beaches and in the highlands in Malaysia, and marveled at the Taj Mahal by moonlight...

The list goes on; play readings, Scottish dancing, taking part in a show for the King of Malaysia, horse riding on racehorses in the tin mines near Kuala Lumpur…and *lots* of music. My mother had trained as a classical pianist and then taught singing at our Primary School in Malaysia. We began piano lessons at an early age and I made some progress despite being a reluctant practicer.

Boarding school.

What I had longed for and joyfully anticipated, fuelled by stories from Lucy who had already done two years there, was, in reality, like of bucket of ice cold water.

Pam and I were still only 10 years old and our parents had just moved to Peking (still not Beijing back then). That first autumn term at our boarding school in England we didn't see them at all and only spoke to them once by long distance telephone. It was a hurried, tense conversation from my grandparents' house with them hovering in the background urging us to be quick. To be fair, a long distance call back then was something of an event and an extremely expensive one at that, but I remember all of us in floods of tears for the rest of the day.

The homesickness was miserable and constant at school. I struggled to fit in but just couldn't get it right.

'Jenny is a very able girl but should learn to be more tolerant of others.' was a frequent comment on my school report card. *'Her bulldozer tactics are not always the wisest way of achieving her object.'*

I was enthusiastic and keen but not good (obviously) at

transmitting that without stepping on toes. Looking back, what was missing for me was loving adult guidance and support, but I was far away from home and just muddled through painfully.

But there was one marvelous thing that I really loved and appreciated about my boarding school- the amount of music and drama that it provided. We put on regular plays, musicals and drama competitions and I reveled in it all. I sang in the school choir which made weekly 'chapel' a joy and continued with piano and singing lessons.

When I was thirteen, for some reason, *I decided to start playing the violin.* My teacher, Sally Brundan, came regularly to the school and I had the good fortune to begin learning with someone who was kind and enthusiastic, and who showered me with encouragement right away. I loved my lessons with her and they had the added advantage of getting me out of double maths once a week. Practice provided me with a legitimate way to be on my own, which is not an easy feat in a boarding school.

The violin suited me. I loved how it felt physically; holding my instrument so close, tucked under my chin, and the sensual feel of drawing the bow across the strings. I loved the sound and thought I sounded just fine (although Pam assured me much later that it was pretty terrible at the beginning!!).

And I loved the emotions that came to me from a place deep inside through the music. Emotions that often seemed quite separate from me, and yet flowed through me, through the nuances of timing and dynamics and tone.

So I made fast progress and was soon leading the school orchestra and going on orchestral and chamber music courses, playing 'catch up' after my late start.

In my last year at boarding school I was travelling an hour and a half up to London once a week (more benefits from playing an instrument) to study privately with the wonderful American violinist Dona Lee Croft. This was heaven for me and I made the most of it, practicing long and hard between classes in order to improve and shine.

I was determined to go to Music College in London. I was advised against aiming for 'just' performance - after my late start it was preferable to do a teaching diploma instead and keep my options open - but I stubbornly held out for performing, knowing that it was what I really loved to do.

I spent a blissful gap year practicing the violin eight hours a day, seven days a week, (though Christmas day I cut down to six hours in honor of the occasion) improving my level and taking final music exams so that I could apply to music college.

Although my playing level was good enough by now, I was woefully unprepared for the questions thrown at me in the initial interviews.

'What do you want to do with your musical career?' 'Which orchestra or group inspires you the most?'

I didn't have a clue. I'd never heard of the concepts of goal-setting or having a vision or being inspired by others. As for 'reaching for the stars' I felt lucky just to be kicking around in the dirt getting a chance to play at ground level.

Still, I got accepted by the Royal College of Music and by Trinity College, both in central London. I chose the latter because I would have the chance to study with the renowned Hungarian violin professor, Bela Katona, who was in the String Department at Trinity.

How differently my life would have turned out if I'd accepted a place at the Royal College instead…

Visit the link below to access the Free Audio Book (read by the author.)

www.jennyclift.com/freeaudiobook

1.3 *Trinity, non-violin years and the first attempt*

I should have known it wasn't going to work. Even before starting that first term at Trinity College I had dented Maestro Katona's Hungarian pride.

Plans had been made in the summer to go and hear Dona Lee Croft play a concerto with an orchestra and she suggested that I offer to take Mr. Katona along in my car for the hour or so ride. He accepted gratefully and all was set.

Then, the night before, I was talking to a close friend, who pointed out that my house was somewhere between Bela's place and the concert venue, and that I should suggest to him that he come first to my house and we go on together in my car. (Oh, it still makes me cringe to write this even 34 years later...) I called him and he seemed perfectly fine as we talked...the next thing I know there was a call from Dona Lee saying that he was very offended and would be travelling alone.

Ouch. How ignorant could I be? And what a way to start our relationship.

Mr. Katona taught many of the star pupils at Trinity and with those top level players he was a fantastic teacher.

But I wasn't ready for him. Not technically and definitely not as an insecure eighteen year old.

His method (with me at least) was to strip all the music out of the process and use dry exercises and scales in an effort to rehabilitate my playing. He was not open to questions and, instead of adapting and cooperating with him, I just shut down and resisted.

He expected me to study for eight hours a day (that magic number again!) and I didn't go near that. I came to dread our lessons and he probably did too. His frustration and disgust at me and my inability to respond to his teaching was increasingly apparent.

At the end of every class he would growl: *'Get on with it.'*

But somehow, despite my love for the violin, despite wanting to improve and despite normally being a good, obedient student, I just couldn't.

Thank goodness I had to play *some* music as part of my Trinity education. I was concertmaster of the Training Orchestra in the first year and I loved that, but I became less and less confident in my abilities as a player, feeling that any status I had at Trinity was just because I was one of Katona's students. I felt that the moment I started playing I'd be discovered for what I thought I was- an imposter, lacking in talent and ability and just there on false pretences.

Little did I know that these negative thoughts and feelings would be the start of a kind of sickness that would take three decades to move through and finally heal.

I avoided socializing with the other students, staying clear of the common room or any kind of college life.

In my mind we were all in competition with each other and *I was losing.* So my strategy was just to keep away, keep all relationships on a very superficial level and not get involved with the student life and the other musicians there.

I stuck it out for three years, increasingly miserable and insecure, hating it more and more. I managed to scrape through the exams and received my Diploma and then, after a few more weeks, I dropped out.

Completely and utterly.

I stopped playing the violin for *eight* years.

But life goes on, so what on earth was I going to do with mine now?

I took a typing course, toyed with the idea of working in a real estate agent's, and then decided, 'OK, I'll travel the world teaching English.' I took a TEFL (Teaching English as a Foreign Language) course and wound up in Salamanca in Spain.

For the next ten years I was an English teacher.

At first I loved teaching, loved the connection with my students, especially the adults, and threw myself into being as creative, enthusiastic and energetic as possible.

I didn't miss the violin or classical music at all. In fact, it was a blessed relief to have nothing to do with that world.

I met the man who was to become my first husband; he was studying to become a doctor, and my social life revolved around him and my work colleagues.

I started to do a lot of yoga - loving the whole body, mind and Spirit aspect of it. I went to movies, cleaned the house a lot (I've never had such clean windows before or since!) and got on with my life.

Although my violin was with me in Spain (sitting in a cupboard gathering dust) I never went near it and I didn't talk to anyone about having trained to become a violinist. *But I always had a feeling in the back of my mind that one day I would get it out again*, even if just as a hobby.

We'd been living in Alicante in the south-east of Spain and I was happy, enjoying my work and the friends I'd made there. Santi and I decided to get married and it looked like things would go on that way for a while.

But a week after our wedding he told me he wanted to move to Madrid as he wanted to take a course totally unrelated to medicine (which he had never been completely in love with.)

I was horrified. I really didn't want to move again away from the friends I had made, the great weather and pleasant lifestyle we had. But he was unhappy in his career and saw this as a way to make a change and find what he really wanted to do with his life.

So I reluctantly agreed to move with him and went up to Madrid for a job interview at a well-known English teaching academy.

Moving to Madrid was yet another turning point for me. This was where I rediscovered music.

I started going to orchestral concerts and that was it. The old longing to be playing was back. I would sit enviously in the audience wishing I was up there with the other musicians on stage.

Eventually after one concert I went backstage and talked to the leader of the orchestra about taking lessons. He put me in touch with a colleague who was happy to take me on as his student.

The Brazilian violinist, Paolo Vieira was exactly what I needed in a violin teacher at that moment. About my age, a methodical, experienced and talented teacher, he was also approachable and friendly. He soon started encouraging me to get back to music and to try performing again, even helping me get a month's contract playing Verdi's opera 'Rigoletto' with his orchestra.

This coincided with my mother coming to live in Madrid with her husband who was posted here as the Norwegian ambassador to Spain. (My parents had separated right around the time I had started at Trinity and had each continued in the diplomatic life with new partners.)

She and I quickly got back to playing violin and piano together and, with Paolo's guidance, started performing in cultural venues in Madrid.

I remember being incredibly nervous and my performances were full of mistakes but it felt good to be putting myself out there again. One concert at the Norwegian embassy led to an opportunity to do a week's work with the Spanish Radio TV orchestra. That went well and I ended up playing regularly as an extra with them over the next four years.

I absolutely loved rehearsing and performing and I'd made it this far so I had to be doing something right on the outside, *but I was still a total mess on the inside.*

When I played in the orchestra I had the strange sensation that I couldn't hear myself in that mass of violins and that I couldn't be heard from the outside either. Which actually suited me because I was convinced I was going to be found out at any moment. Someone had to notice that *I* wasn't a professional.

I still felt like an insecure teenager playing with the grownups, without any real right to be there. Any tiny slip on my part led to hours of berating myself for my incompetence.

My inner critic was having a field day.

I held up OK in the orchestra and there was definitely the feeling of 'safety in numbers'. But stand me up on my own in an audition to try and get accepted permanently in the orchestra and I was a quivering jelly.

I did some work with a fellow musician and friend to help my stage fright, but only from a technical standpoint using a sort of 'desensitization' method, which involved recording myself and examining my performances.

I also read 'Feel the Fear and Do it Anyway' by Susan Jeffers, which was brilliant.

But I didn't go anywhere near the underlying emotions, fears and feelings. I didn't try to heal them and clear them. How could I? I didn't know that that was what I needed.

So I did it again. I backed off again for another ten years…

Visit the link below to access 2 Free Mp3 Audios ('Danny Boy' and 'The Flowers of Edinburgh' played by the Laurus Freestyle Duo. Jenny Clift, violin and Cy Williams, guitar.)

www.jennyclift.com/freemp3laurus1

1.4 Teaching years

But this time I didn't back off so completely. This time I was at least teaching violin and was involved with music on a daily basis (if you can call playing Twinkle Twinkle for the hundredth time music!)

This time I was also performing. At first I joined a string quartet which led to a handful of concerts in and around Madrid and to close friendships with my fellow players. It's hard to cry with laughter when you are rehearsing Beethoven's late string quartets but we somehow managed it!

At the weekends I started working as an interpreter for specialist music courses at the local University of Alcalá de Henares just outside of Madrid. It was good to make use of my fluent Spanish and I was the only one who minded my English accent!

At one of these weekend courses I met an incredible American violin teacher, Mimi Zweig, a professor at the Indiana School of Music and one of the first teachers of Joshua Bell (the amazing American violinist). I immersed myself in her teaching methods (also benefitting my own playing) to the extent of going out to Indiana to help with her annual Summer School.

When I got back I felt much more confident in my teaching methods and strategies and threw myself into this field with enthusiasm. I found work in several different private music academies and international schools in Madrid and gradually built my experience and student numbers.

I found my niche in a small, but extremely successful, English school on the outskirts of Madrid. They took students from three years old right through to eighteen and, although the school was more academically orientated, they understood the need to provide private instrumental teaching to those parents who wanted this extra-curricular activity for their children.

Over the years I turned this from a handful of students into a fulltime job. I was squeezing in students between their regular school classes and literally squeezing into corridors and borrowed classrooms, even broom cupboards.

I was basically my own boss, which suited me fine, although I was extremely fortunate to be there at the same time as a wonderful Head of Music and an extremely supportive Director of the Primary school.

I taught myself how to balance the books and chase up late payers (not my favorite activity) as well as teach the children and put on twice yearly shows for their parents.

For many years I loved it. I too was learning about the violin with its many technical challenges and I had a lot of fun with my different students.

Through my colleagues in the string quartet I was invited to play with a local orchestra. This was made up mainly of music teachers like me so we rehearsed at the weekends and played concerts about once a month. After a couple of concerts the Conductor asked me to be the leader and I accepted gladly.

I loved leading. I loved being right there in the centre of things. I loved the solos that the role of concertmaster required me to play from time to time, and I loved the camaraderie. We weren't being paid much, just a token amount for 'expenses', so everyone was there for the same reason- they wanted to play and to perform great music. My desk partner (the person I regularly sat next to) became a close friend as did many other of the musicians I was working with.

So, *for many years I was totally satisfied and convinced that I was doing what I would do for the rest of my working life.*

Those years also coincided with meeting my current husband. My first marriage had fallen apart right around the time I was auditioning for several orchestras and we had realized that we were poles apart and that we wanted different things, both personally and professionally.

This new relationship was a total contrast. We were each pursuing our own careers (his in Human Resources) but supporting and encouraging each other.

After a few years we decided to have children and had a daughter and then, two and a half years later, twin girls. Quite unexpected, with shades of 'Il ya une autre', although I discovered I was carrying my two at my six week scan and not at the birth! I loved having the girls and jumped happily into the mothering role - enjoying my time off from both teaching and performing during their early months.

Going back to school after having the twins was much harder than I'd anticipated. Now I was looking after toddlers at home and then teaching little children during the daytime and I found it exhausting, both physically and mentally.

The orchestra was different. That was my escape valve. When the other members (nearly all of them significantly younger than me) complained about giving up their weekend to rehearse, I would think, *'Oh, this is a holiday compared to raising three children.'* Although I loved getting back to my daughters it was also wonderful to have some time off too. I'm sure a lot of parents will understand!

I never stopped studying the violin. I have always had weekly or bi-weekly lessons and fit in time to practice in order to learn and advance as a player. Much slower than I would have liked, but at least I wasn't getting stagnant.

Through my teacher at the time I met a Dutch pianist who accompanied me in a Master class. We immediately hit if off both musically and personally and a few weeks later she called me to say that she and her husband (a viola player) were looking for a violinist to form a piano quartet and asked if I would like to join them. I was thrilled. The string quartet I'd played with before had folded when we all started having babies and I missed the intimacy and autonomy of playing in a chamber group, not to mention the incredibly beautiful repertoire that exists for small ensembles.

I rearranged my schedule and we started rehearsing on Monday mornings. What a blissful start to the week.

My feeling was that now, with the orchestra and the quartet, I would be totally satisfied as a performing musician and could do the teaching as a way of making a living.

Except it didn't quite work out like that.

The more I was playing and performing, the more I wanted to spend my time doing just that, and the more I resented being away from my own studying when I had to focus on my students. I continued to find teaching the older children the most rewarding. But starting off with new beginners and searching for ways to motivate reluctant practisers was becoming more and more challenging.

The rot was starting to set in…

I had begun to do some inner work, mainly reading and journaling.

After completing 'Feel the Fear' (which, by the way, introduced me to the very best Gratitude exercise I have ever used - more about that in my later chapter on 'Writing'), I then went through all of M. Scott Peck's 'The Road Less Travelled' books, Alan Cohen's books, especially 'The Dragon doesn't live here Any

More', Wayne Dyer's 'The Erroneous Zones' and Louise Hay's 'You Can Heal Your Life'.

Combining inner work with music, one of my favorite books was (and still is) 'The Inner Game of Music' by Barry Green and Timothy Gallwey. I even got to do a course with Barry in Alcalá.

I never thought of any of this as 'self-help' or even 'personal development', I just found all of these books fascinating to read. (See Part 5, Chapter 1 for links to all these people and books.)

I was very attracted to the idea of being personally responsible for my life and of making changes within myself to improve things outside.

A turning point came when I was on holiday one summer with my family.

We rented a big house altogether - about 15 of us -in the beautiful countryside near Bath in the south of England.

Coming through the airport on my arrival from Spain I'd picked up, totally at random, a copy of a book called *'Change Your Life in Seven Days' by Paul McKenna*. I was drawn more to the author than the title (although that was enticing too) as he is a well-known British hypnotist with many books on different subjects.

I've always been fascinated by hypnotism and had even been to a hypnotist once when I was trying to get pregnant the first time. It was taking a long time (I was almost certainly trying too hard!) and I looked up a local hypnotist when I was visiting my twin sister back in Britain. I made an appointment and had a session which was one of the most relaxing experiences I'd ever had. I then listened to the audio he'd given me regularly for a few weeks and very soon afterwards was expecting. And then twins two and a half years later… which pretty much sold me on the whole technique.

So, on holiday with my family back in the summer of 2010, I would go out early every morning and sit in my car under a blanket (August can be cold in England) as the only available CD player was there, and listen to Paul's hypnosis tape. I read right through the book and did all the exercises that he suggested.

This book, and another of Paul's books, 'I Can Make You Thin', introduced me to two things, which were to become important keys in making changes in my life. One, the Law of Attraction (based on the maxims 'like attracts like' and 'what you focus on expands') and two, EFT or 'Tapping'.

In retrospect, that book really did change my life.

Those seven days started me moving in a whole new direction which was to result in a lot of changes in a relatively short space of time…

In these chapters I've explained how I got to this turning point in my life. In the next chapter I will tell you how I started using EFT, what exactly it is and how it can be used to start clearing the inner blocks and obstacles which are keeping you from going for what you really want in life.

Visit the link below to access 2 Free Mp3 Audios ('Gymnopedie 1' by E. Satie and 'Crossfire' by C. Williams played by the Laurus Freestyle Duo; Jenny Clift, violin and Cy Williams, guitar.)

www.jennyclift.com/freemp3laurus2

Part 2
Tap to Change

2.1 EFT

'Keep calm and keep tapping.'

For many years Pam, my twin sister, had been urging me to learn how to use a computer. I'd resisted, spending my time practicing the violin and doing all my book-keeping for my teaching practice in little notebooks, doing all my work sheets and writing by hand, and using the photocopier at school. I had no interest and no time (or so I thought) to learn how to use this 'monster' that sat in the corner of our living-room.

But now everything had changed. I wanted access to more information about the new ideas that had been introduced to me through Paul McKenna's book.

It didn't take me too long to discover YouTube.

Hard to imagine not knowing about it, isn't it? Especially as a musician. I quickly realized that I could access millions of amazing recordings by incredible artists. I also started watching videos about the Law of Attraction (I'd learnt that name by now) and related topics.

One name started popping up over and over: Abraham Hicks. After about four months I decide to investigate this 'person'.

Wow, that certainly introduced me to a whole new world.

A world of channeling messages (Esther Hicks is the 'spokeswoman' for an entity named 'Abraham') and speaking of concepts such as 'creating your own reality'. I hung in there even though it felt quite 'far out'!

I was attracted to their messages of focusing on the positive, taking responsibility for my life (and not blaming others), moving up the emotional scale, asking, allowing and creating with 'deliberate intent'.

I bought a lot of their books and religiously (though I know it is not a religion, let's get that quite clear) did the exercises for feeling better and starting to 'create my own reality'. They were fun and I kept at them - but they had a nasty side effect.

I found myself growing angrier and angrier.

Angrier at school, angrier at home, even angrier in the orchestra when the other players chatted constantly instead of 'getting on with it'.

(Oh, I knew that would come back to haunt me some day!)

I found myself getting into a downward emotional spiral and now I could add *guilt* to my list of negative emotions because now I knew too that it was *all my fault*.

Great. So much for the Law of Attraction.

Luckily, one day while watching an Abraham video about being 'In the Vortex' I noticed a related video, 'Allowing Vortex' by an English guy named David Childerley.

In his introduction he explained that he used a technique known as EFT, short for 'Emotional Freedom Technique', or simply 'tapping'.

He then started saying sentences which I had to repeat back (I was on my own at home so no one was there to ask what on earth I was doing) while tapping on different parts of my face and torso.

Yes, good job I was alone…although for some reason it didn't look at all strange to me, it was just interesting.

And as I checked out other videos I liked what I was hearing more and more.

Because instead of going straight for the positive -'I am a calm, happy, successful, wonderful person.' -which felt totally unbelievable, he started out by saying the magic words…

'Even though I'm stuck, angry, a horrible person, fill in the blanks, say it how you really mean it…

I choose to love and accept myself.'

What? I'm stuck, angry, horrible and even worse…and can still love and accept myself? This was a turn up for the books! No, strike that. *This was revolutionary.*

And as the words went on and I continued to tap I was able to finish up with positive statements that actually felt true. I was genuinely feeling a lot better.

I learnt the phrase *'What you resist persists'* back then and realized that that was what I had been doing, big time. When I had tried to stop being angry it had just resulted in more anger. When I attempted to be less self-critical I found myself mentally beating myself up even more.

Once I accepted these awful emotions and feelings and realized I was able to accept myself- well then I was able to start letting them go.

I surfed and surfed. I found Gary Craig, who was the founder of EFT, and read all about what it is and how it had started.

In a nutshell, EFT is based on the Chinese meridian energy system, which assumes that every physical body has an energy system flowing in and around it. When that energy flow gets interrupted or blocked, the body experiences physical or emotional un-wellness. Clearing the energy to get it moving again will help you to heal and feel better. In acupuncture the clearing is achieved by sticking needles into different points but in EFT you use two or more fingers and tap on different places.

(In case you are starting to snort, there are now scientific studies showing that this process dramatically lowers cortisol levels (what is referred to as the 'stress' hormone), as well as volumes of anecdotal evidence.)

Although the full 'procedure' involves many points and even includes humming and rolling your eyes, now many practitioners simplify the process to use the following points:

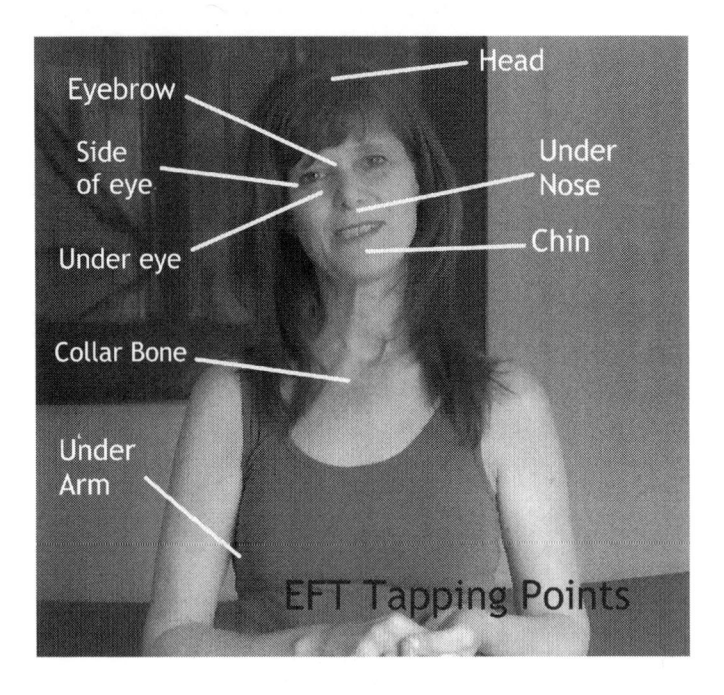

Before starting to tap, it is standard practice to identify the 'upset' and rate it on a scale of 1-10. That could be any number of things: 'Anger at Bob', 'Headache', 'Stage fright' etc.

Then you tap round the points saying phrases that keep you focused on the issue at hand (literally), normally beginning with the 'negative' and moving to more 'positive' as you go through.

At the end you take another reading of how you are feeling and then either tap again, on the same or related issues, (as they say, it's like 'peeling the layers of an onion') until you experience relief.

EFT is used for all manner of things, such as addictions,

cravings, phobias, PTSD (Post Traumatic Stress Disorder), pain and disease, weight loss, removing or alleviating negative emotions and implementing positive goals. To name just a few.

> Visit the link below for my Free Video 'Introduction to EFT'.
>
> *www.jennyclift.com/freeEFTvideo*

As a performer I was immediately struck by the possibilities of this technique for dealing with all the different aspects involved.

Aspects such as performance anxiety, self-doubt, physical blocks and injuries, bad days and difficult lessons.

On Gary Craig's website I discovered many articles from EFT practitioners who had used the technique specifically with musicians as well as with sportsmen and women, and dancers.

The articles had titles like:

> 'Using EFT to conquer jitters for musicians.'
> 'EFT brings about 80.7% sports performance improvement.'
> 'Clearing an old issue helps jazz singer improvise.'
> 'How do I apply EFT for performance issues?'

This was gold. I read and read, getting more and more excited.

As I continued to surf I discovered many other great EFT practitioners such as Carol Look, Andy Bryce, Gary Williams (who runs the EFT 'Hub'), Margaret Lynch, Dawson Church, and Nick and Jessica Ortner. All these people were brilliantly covering many different areas in which EFT was, and is, proving to be invaluable. (Check them out in 'Links and Furthur Reading'.)

I started tapping in earnest.

And then I stumbled upon Brad Yates.

It wasn't very hard to find him, actually, as he had about four hundred free tapping (EFT) videos up on YouTube (six hundred at the time of writing this book in 2015). They covered pretty much anything- very much in line with Gary Craig's catch phrase of *'Try it on everything'*. I really enjoyed his style; humorous, but very down to earth, compassionate and kind.

It was very much what I wanted and needed.

After a little while of tapping along with his videos and checking out his website, I decided to buy one of his programs, entitled *'Belief Beyond Belief'*. (Check out the chapter towards the end of this book on 'Inspiration' for information about this and other online courses.)

This was the first time I had ever bought an online program and I immediately messed up after the payment, failing to click on the 'return to merchant' button (despite it being big and yellow!) and therefore was not able to access my download links. Duh.

I sent him an email and he replied a few hours later solving the problem.

I listened –and tapped- through the 'Belief' program, struck by all the different things coming up for the participants and how doing the EFT rounds with Mr. Yates allowed them to let go of these beliefs and move forward in a totally different state of mind.

By now I was hooked. Here was a process that I could use to address all the things coming up for me, fast and furiously, as I contemplated changing my life.

Address them, examine them through different eyes, and then clear them. Wow!

After a few more weeks I decided to take an even more daring step and contact Brad about doing a private session by Skype. (New lesson for me: How to download Skype.)

In my first email I explained a little about wanting to move into performing.

He replied the next day (I *like* quick workers, getting off to a good start here) with a list of his available times and a form to complete to give him some initial information about me and what I wanted out of this session together.

This is part of what I put in the form:

> 'I want to move into more performing, I always wanted to get into a fulltime professional orchestra and my goal would be to be the leader.
>
> Anger management- especially with children, both at home and in my teaching. (EFT is definitely helping with this already.)
>
> Better use of the Law of Attraction.'

In the part which asked 'What would your ideal life look like? And what thoughts and feelings come up about why you believe that it can't be that way? Rate these beliefs on a scale of 1 to 10, 10 being' I totally believe it', 1 being 'I don't believe that at all'.' I put:

> "I am so happy and grateful now that I am married to a really good man, have three beautiful, healthy daughters and work in music, playing and teaching the violin. I suppose I would say that my life's purpose would be somehow using the violin and music to spread joy- both to myself and to other people. For me the biggest thrill of all is performing and I would like to be doing more of that and ultimately leading an orchestra. (Thoughts and feelings coming up: 'No way', 'I'm not good enough', 'too old' and 'haven't got the right qualifications'. Rated at 8 (on a scale of 1-10).)
>
> As a mother I would like to be able to help my daughters be happy and successful and to find their 'thing' to achieve fulfillment. I would also like to get less angry. (Thoughts and beliefs: 'I get so angry when they don't cooperate'. Rated at 8.)
>
> I am grateful that I have enough money for my needs; I would like to have enough so that career decisions don't have

to be based on finances -I feel a bit stuck in the teaching because it brings in the money. (Thoughts and beliefs:'There isn't much money in performing'. 8) ('I can't imagine having LOADS of money.' 'I'm not desperate enough to attract a lot more.' 8.)

I would like to teach fewer students and attract students who really want to learn, who are willing to practice and who enjoy working with me. (Beliefs: 'If I was a better teacher I would have better students.' 7.)

In our very first session we talked - and tapped - about my concerns about playing badly in a master class that I had coming up at the end of the week and about not *letting* myself play better. Brad finished the session with a mini hypnosis, what he calls a guided imagery, about imagining myself playing beautifully and effortlessly. That felt really good.

The master class that Friday went much better than I had been anticipating. I now wanted to continue this process for a little while at least. I could see I had plenty to work on.

Our sessions have continued to this day, though they are now fewer and further between than they used to be. I have also been to several of Brad's workshops (another first for me in 'personal development') and taken part in his group calls, all of which have allowed me to hear what comes up for other people.

I always ask myself, not *'Is this relevant to me?'* but rather *'How is this relevant to me?'* and it is amazing how the mind makes connections, allowing me to clear a lot of issues that I didn't even know I had!

Using Emotional Freedom Technique over the years I have been enabled and freed up emotionally (as the name says) to do things that I just couldn't do before.

Like calling myself an Artist (note the capital letter), having my own business cards and website (oh, those took *a lot* of tapping), making my own CDs, making all the changes in my work situation, and getting into a new orchestra and even into new areas (such as writing a book.)

I have also met a lot of great new people and made many good friends through EFT, none of them any weirder or whackier than me. (Which is 'not at all', FYI!)

So this was – and is - my tool of choice for dealing with difficult emotions and limiting beliefs.

> Visit the link below for 3 free PDFs: EFT Set up Phrases, Tapping Round Instructions and a 21 Day Plan for Forming a Tapping Habit!
>
> www.jennyclift.com/freeEFTpdfs

In this chapter I have explained what EFT is; its history, how it works and what it has done for me and can do for you by clearing any obstacles or limiting beliefs that may be stopping us from moving into the career of our dreams.

And now it is time to go deeper into examining exactly what I think limiting beliefs are, and discussing some of the ones that were the most troublesome for me, many of which I've learned are very common for a lot of people…

2.2 'What's stopping you?' - Limiting beliefs

As we saw in the last chapter, EFT is all about healing by changing our beliefs and clearing our blocks. In this chapter I examine what beliefs are and especially *limiting* beliefs. I talk about how and when they are created and why we hold onto them and resist changing them even when we know they are holding us back.

'That's my story and I'm sticking to it.'
— Brad Yates

The Oxford Dictionary lists the following definitions for the word 'Belief':

1. An acceptance that something exists or is true, especially one without proof.
2. Something one accepts as true or real; a firmly held opinion.
3. A religious conviction.
4. Trust, faith.

Let's examine these definitions.

Definition #1: *'An acceptance that something exists or is true, especially one without proof.'*

Hmm, how many times do we accept something as gospel without ever really thinking about it? Or, even more subtly, how many times do we create (consciously or unconsciously) evidence or proof that something is true, just because we humans 'love to be right.' ?

Think about someone that you know (or knew if that person was in your past.) Say a work colleague or relatively new acquaintance. Maybe you like this person well enough but a friend of yours really doesn't like them at all.

Well, as we know, relationships are all about chemistry; so the signals you are putting out are going to elicit a different response than the signals your friend is putting out. The signals are positive in your case, and negative in theirs. The responses you get are going to reflect those differing signals…and 'ta daa', you've both just created more 'evidence' to support each of your cases. (This is where you and your friend would probably agree to disagree or just change the subject!)

This is easy to understand when it involves people and relationships, but try to stretch your mind just a little bit further and you'll see that this can be applied to circumstances and events too.

Definition #2: *'A firmly held opinion.'*

Belief is just that, an opinion. And where did that opinion come from? It came from observing and listening to the people around you, and has been developing since you were a child. Initially these opinions were largely influenced by your parents, but they can't be 'blamed' for everything! Our opinions come from all of our experiences and many people play a role in their formation.

Think about your teachers, your friends and siblings, community leaders and politicians, the media, religious leaders, pop stars and even just the community around you?

When I first moved to Spain I was bemused (and, yes, a little judgmental) to see tiny children awake and partying at one or two in the morning. Well, that is 'just not done' in England. I remember thinking to myself, *'My God, they must be worn out...' 'They should be fast asleep in bed by now; they'll be exhausted in the morning.'* Or, *'This is adult time, what are they doing up still?'*

But, you know what? In the morning they were just fine. They either slept a little later or recouped with a 'siesta' later in the day; and the adults didn't mind them being up. It was what was normal and natural, so it just wasn't a problem.

We adapt to our own environment and it's easy to assume that *our* way is the right way. We assume what's good for us must be good for others. And naturally, our benchmark for 'normal' and 'right' is ourselves. Crazy, when you stop to think about it.

This craziness gets even more crazy, and sometimes downright dangerous when you look at the next definition.

Definition #3: *'A religious conviction'.*

The more convinced you are of something, the less you are able to see and accept another person's point of view. Which, as we can tell from past *and* present events, can lead to a whole lot of trouble, misery and bloodshed.

Definition #4: *'Trust, faith.'*

For some this can sound like the most comforting thing in the world or as if you've been 'sold a bill of goods', promised something that doesn't deliver. It all depends to what extent you believe that you are *supported by the Universe* (God, Spirit, Allah, whatever term you like to use.)

Albeit a great resource, the Oxford Dictionary is not all encompassing. The following definition for 'beliefs' leaves us with more room for maneuvering:
'Thoughts you think over and over.'
Interesting, huh? Let's read that again:
'Thoughts you think over and over.'
There's no implication here that these thoughts are right or true. Nor is there any suggestion that they are beneficial or detrimental to the person holding them. No, they're just repeated thoughts or ideas which become part of a deeply held belief system. This belief system then influences one's decision to take, or very often *not* to take, certain actions. And these actions lead to certain results.

'Deeply held' is an important phrase here because so often these thoughts are not even in our conscious mind which helps to explain why these beliefs can be so hard to shift.

And, you may ask, why would we want to shift them anyway?

That question leads us on to the topic of 'limiting beliefs', which are, just as the name suggests, beliefs ('Thoughts you think over and over' remember?) that limit you. **Limit what you consider you can do, be and have, and which take you out of the game before it's even started.**

We all have them.

I consider myself to have lived a relatively normal life so far (ha ha, remember that benchmark?). Nothing too horrible in my past.

And yet, I was (past tense) full of limiting beliefs.

And when do these limiting beliefs show up the most? They don't usually show up when you are deciding which channel to watch or whether to have pepperoni or margarita pizza for dinner (though they can of course!). Instead they are more likely to come when you are contemplating stepping out of what feels comfortable and doing something new, something challenging and a bit scary, something that forces you to 'put yourself out there' and learn and grow.

Things like changing your career, or looking for a life partner or posting on Facebook (nah, just kidding about FB...*or am I?*)

That's when they come up *big* time.

'I'm too old.' 'I'm not good enough.' 'What will 'they' think?' 'There's no way I can do that.' 'Who am I to...?' 'That's just not me.'

And on and on and on...

But! Get this. None of them are *true*. They are just thoughts and we can reprogram our thoughts. We can change our minds and start to believe something different.

You may now be thinking: 'It's not that easy.' (See what just popped up. Another limiting belief...sorry, I couldn't resist!)

Don't worry. I totally agree with you there.

But why is it so difficult?

It's alright for Rumi, the thirteenth century Persian mystic, who once asked: '*Why do you stay in prison when the door is so wide open?*'

Well, Rumi, partly because of what I've talked about. That these beliefs are often so deeply buried that we are not even aware of them. So we can't even see a door, let alone notice that it is open.

Have you ever had the experience of being with a friend and discussing a movie that you have just both seen and realizing that you may as well have seen completely different movies? Your memories are different and the points and conclusions you come to are different.

Why is this? Because **we see, hear and experience things with our filters firmly in place**. We literally do not see, hear and experience that which is *not* safe (according to our inner programming).

So even if we could see Rumi's door we can only begin to

imagine all the frightening monsters that would jump out at us if we walked through that door. It just doesn't feel safe to change our thinking.

Remember my violin professor at Trinity snarling at me at the end of every class: *'Get on with it'*?

I knew rationally that he was right, that I had to 'get on with it'. I had to practice those exercises and scales, make all those minute changes, all with the aim of improving my skill and technique…

I knew it, and yet, *I couldn't do it.*

I was still in this place about twenty-five years later, living here in Spain, and studying with another violin teacher. He told me to hold my bow arm higher to improve the sound. He told me this about once a week for about two years.

And I still couldn't do it.

Why not? Was it laziness ('too much effort') or sheer bloody-mindedness (even though I felt bloody-minded towards yet another teacher, I could see that the technique worked for other violinists) or a physical limitation (Doctor's note: 'Jenny has unnaturally weak muscles in her right arm. Please do not ask her to force them in any way.)?

No, none of these. Because the second I cleared out the limiting belief of 'I can't hold my right arm higher when I'm playing the violin' (by tapping on it in an EFT session with my coach) I was able to do so easily. My violin teacher even commented in the following lesson that I could be holding my arm a little *too* high!

I have never been troubled by that particular technical hitch since.

So what was my 'safety issue' here? The immediate one was that I felt physically more vulnerable with my right arm lifted up (it felt like anyone could take a shot at me) but I later came to believe that it was a much more deep-rooted fear than that.

My mentor and Life Coach, Brad Yates, is fond of saying:

'Self-sabotage is misguided self-love.'

So you see, you are not trying to *harm* yourself when you

procrastinate, or when you eat that extra doughnut or fail to return the application form for that orchestral audition in time.

No, a part of you is looking after you. It knows what is safe for you, or thinks it does, and it brilliantly stops you from doing whatever might take you out of the safety zone (sometimes known as your comfort zone, although it is very often far from comfortable.)

But, here's the good news. **It may be difficult to change your limiting beliefs but it is NOT impossible.** I know from my experience… and you know too, from your own experience and from seeing other people take risks and become successful.

It takes a little digging, a little rethinking and a little time (sometimes more, sometimes less, than you expect) but it is definitely possible.

Before moving on to discuss further tools and techniques that have helped me with the digging and which helped me make so many changes in my own thinking, I'd like to share some limiting beliefs which I feel are common to many of us and to show you how I changed them from *limiting* **beliefs to** *liberating* **beliefs**.

2.3 *Limiting beliefs to liberating beliefs*

My thinking has changed radically over the last few years around a number of limiting beliefs, allowing me to transform them into what I think of as *liberating* beliefs. In this chapter I will share thirteen of these limiting beliefs with you, ones which were particularly predominant for me as I tried to move into the career that I really desired.

Some of these beliefs I clung to stubbornly, some I was able to let go of quickly and relatively painlessly and some I'm still working on…there's still more digging to be done on this particular archeological site!

I present them to you in no particular order. They appeared as I worked on myself inwardly. I'm sure many will sound very familiar and you will also have a few of your own which haven't come up for me (yet.)

#1 'I'm too old.'

Leading up to my fiftieth birthday, this one was huge for me.

Although I didn't talk about it much, for my entire forty- ninth year I was inwardly obsessed with my age. Sometimes in a more cheerful way; 'Well, at least I don't look fifty', and sometimes (often) less so. 'I've left everything too late.'

Which brought in the 'And I started the violin much too late.'

Also 'How could I have not taken advantage of all those opportunities I had in the past to become a performer?'

Add extra ammunition: 'How on earth am I going to get to a professional level now? All those brilliant players out there are under *thirty*. I screwed up way back then and now it is much too late.'

Then one day my Life Coach quoted a Chinese proverb to me:

'The best time to plant a tree is twenty years ago. The second best time is now.'

And that suddenly hit home. Yes, all of my beliefs may be 'true', but does that even matter? I might not be able to get into the Berlin Philharmonic Orchestra (who according to my violin teacher at the time weren't taking anyone over the age of thirty, and, who knows, even that might not be the case anymore) but does that mean that all openings to perform, or to play professionally, are closed to me because of my age? Well no, not at all.

There is no one else stopping me. It's just that pesky voice in my head (yes, yes, trying to keep me safe, I know, yawn, yawn…)

So what if I'm old enough to be everyone's mother in the orchestra I'm now playing with? Most of them don't know that (I'm keeping mum!)

And in so many ways I *love* being older. I am much more confident, and much wiser than I used to be. I have more highly developed social skills and am not afraid to be friendly and outgoing, thinking that I might be seen as being pushy or out of place, which is how I used to feel. I don't 'need' anything from the other musicians. After all, I have a wonderful husband and three gorgeous children and I feel secure in what I am aiming for musically and professionally.

And I've now come to believe, quite genuinely, that this is all part of a grand master plan- that my life took all those twists and turns, instead of being a straight 'Roman road', for a distinct reason which I am only starting to glimpse at now.

#2 'I'm not good enough.'

Oh, this is such a showstopper. Really totally meaningless, but it keeps us grounded and miserable and unable to move into a better place.

This is a real 'evidence'- based belief.

As a musician, how many notes have I missed? Millions. How many auditions and exams have I messed up? Plenty. How many times have I proved to myself- and others- that my technique is, at best, unreliable, and at worst, downright horrible? Can't count that far…

A couple of years ago I played a piece 'a capella' to some of my private students and their parents at the end of one of the concerts that I organize periodically for them to get together and practice performing. It was a piece I knew really well, had played countless times perfectly adequately, and I made a terrible mess of it. From the first note I felt insecure, stiff and awkward and it didn't improve all the way through.

What was that all about? It couldn't possibly be that I had an orchestral audition coming up a few weeks later and that I just had to convince myself in advance that this was a really bad idea, that I was definitely not good enough. Or could it…?

And you know what? I bet if I had the chance to interview the legendary violinist Paganini (long dead, so, unless I start channeling, no chance of that!), he would have been on top of himself for the things he hadn't mastered yet instead of being amazed and empowered by what he already could do.

There are always new things to learn; it's what keeps us alive and creating. And so long as it's someone else who is trying out new things, who is taking risks, messing up and getting back in the saddle, then we admire them and look up to them.

Look at Elvis Presley who was told: 'You ain't goin' nowhere, son. You ought to go back to drivin' a truck.'

Look at Vincent van Gogh who sold only one painting during his life.

Look at Stephen King who submitted his first novel 'Carrie' thirty times and was rejected thirty times. He threw it out but luckily his wife rescued it from the trash and encouraged him to give it just one more try.

And how about Albert Einstein who had speech difficulties as a child and was even once thought to be mentally handicapped?

Thank goodness these people didn't give up because they weren't 'good enough'.

But we allow *ourselves* to give up. We say 'Oh, Elvis (Vincent, Stephen, Albert) is different. I'm nothing special.'

You know the real difference between them and us? They probably also had their moments of despair, of self-doubt and feeling that they weren't good enough. After all, they were (are) all human.

But somehow they didn't have the same blocks. Or they were able to clear those blocks or bypass them to an extent that left them with a way to move forward and allow their genius to show through. (And in Stephen's case he had a smart wife!!)

I truly believe (and this is a very liberating belief) that there is genius and talent in *all* of us. How can it be otherwise? Not only are we good enough, we *all* have the potential to star, to inspire and to lead the way, if only we can let go of our fears and our limiting ideas.

Which ties right into limiting belief

#3 'I'm not talented enough.' (Otherwise known as 'Who am I to…?')

Violinists. Check them out on YouTube. Nathan Milstein, Jascha Heifetz, Anne Sophie Mutter, Gil Shaham, Hilary Hahn, Kyung Wah Chung, Joshua Bell…the list goes on and on. There are thousands of them. And they are all so good. Astounding technique, incredible musicality, wonderful stage presence…Talent.

And me? Li'l ole me? Who the heck am I to acknowledge that I'm talented, to dedicate time and effort to developing my skills, to make recordings and put them out there?

I think this shrinking, this putting ourselves down instead of building ourselves up, comes from countless messages as we are growing up: 'Don't show off.' 'Sit down and shut up!' 'Children should be seen and not heard (and preferably not even seen).' 'What makes you think you're so special?'

Or even just receiving disapproving and shaming looks or humiliating laughter. All these are ways of squashing any spark, any signs of wanting to step out and stand out in any way.

Sometimes this is done cruelly and with seemingly ill-intent (by people who have suffered similar discouragement and putdowns).

But, I think, more often it happens because people have their own fears and limitations and so they unconsciously do two things. First, they are trying to keep you safe in their own misguided way, and second, this serves as a way of justifying their own choices which were *based on their own fears.*

Remember those past mentors who advised me to take the 'smart path' and pursue teaching rather than performing? I can recall one pointing out; 'Violin soloists start when they are three years old, not thirteen.'

I realize now that they were just trying to protect me from being hurt and disappointed in the future… *but was it also a subconscious attempt to justify their own choices?* Just maybe, they too had always dreamed of performing but had stopped themselves from doing something that felt unsafe, and stuck to teaching.

Actually, it's a bit of a miracle that anyone gets anywhere – an indication that growth and expansion and learning is an inherent part of all of us.

In my case, I knew that technically my violin skills still had a long way to go. (They still do. As I said before, we can always improve and develop.)

But I also knew that I felt music very deeply. That there seemed to be a strong impulse inside me that directed me how to finish a certain phrase, how to time the music, how to ask for particular dynamics and nuances in order for that voice to come through.

I thought everyone had it. What I realize now is that everyone does, but in their own field, their own area of passionate interest.

As for the whole 'showing off' issue, three things helped me with it directly.

The first was to call it *'showing up'* instead of showing off. Showing up; being fully present, giving one hundred percent, being professional and responsible and really there in whatever activity I am undertaking.

Another was (is) to think of myself as *a 'channel' for music*. As I have mentioned before, this was at first a little 'woo-woo' for my practical mindset, but now it makes total sense to me and allows me to disconnect from the idea of ego, of somehow being better or more special than others because of my 'amazing talent'. After all, it really does feel like something separate from me but inside me. I found that as I allowed myself to recognize that I do have talent for interpreting music, then I could also allow myself to improve my technical skills much faster. Not at quantum speed (I'm not that evolved yet) but much faster than ever before.

And the third thing was something my Life Coach said to me.

That *we each have a unique voice*, and that my way of performing a particular piece of music might not appeal to everybody, but it might just be the one interpretation that opens a person's ears to the music, allowing them to really hear it for the first time.

And he finished off by saying; *'The question is not 'Who are you to do this?' But, 'Who are you* not *to?'*

#4 'There aren't any jobs/opportunities out there.'

When I decided to leave my teaching post one of my huge fears was that 'there aren't enough jobs or orchestral positions or opportunities out there.' The economy in Spain in 2013 was a mess and it seemed that all people could talk about was the difficulty of finding work, the lack of openings out there, how badly paid everyone was, how everyone had stopped going to concerts etc.

I had thought that when I eventually made the move jobwise it would be because I already had another position lined up, that it would be a smooth and easy transition with people congratulating me left, right and centre.

Actually it was a lot more untidy than that. To be honest I felt like a 'spoiled brat' and didn't mention this career move to many, many people until quite a few months later, a year in some cases.

I went through so many emotions, chiefly fear and shame, but also sadness at having built up so much only to now knock it all down again.

The opportunities and the jobs didn't come until a bit later. I spent those lean months learning – in fact I have come to consider 'quiet' periods as 'Lean Learning Times' and to use them to spend time on my inner work and on improving my technical skills.

Little by little, opportunities started to show up. I found that they often did so by indirect routes.

Like making free videos to put up on YouTube which led

to being contacted by an online education site, Curious.com, and eventually to me making two courses, 'Violin for Adult Beginners' and 'Christmas Music', and being paid $1,000 for them up front.

There were also shots in the dark. Under one of Paul Santisi's amazing 3D meditations (also on YouTube!) I read a little note saying 'We're looking for musicians to form MusicMastermind'. The other performers seemed to be in other genres; hip-hop, rap and the like, and I was sure that my email was destined straight for 'file under bin'. So I was amazed when Paul got back to me with great enthusiasm and interest. A Skype call led to a contract to make recordings and to an interview – and that's just the beginning.

There's also been a lot of hard work and pushing through my fears of contacting (read bothering) people. Phoning and emailing representatives and concert venues, and setting up gigs for my violin and guitar duo. We did a lot of freebies at the beginning and had a few, well, let's say, interesting experiences, but also many, many wonderful paid concerts where we were able to sell our CDs and get our music out there to more and more people.

I still dislike sending emails off into the blue and then having to wait for what feels like an eternity for a reply- sometimes up to a year later and sometimes never!

(I love that joke:
'Can we set up an appointment? How's next Wednesday looking?'
'Next Wednesday? Hmm, let me see…How about never? How's never for you?')

I've had to learn not to take it personally, not to become discouraged or see it as something wrong with myself or my music or that I'm being a nuisance.

It gets easier…

I would say that the main thing is to persist, not give up.

I have just signed a contract with a professional orchestra, here in my hometown of Madrid, to play with them for the 2015/16 season. (About sixty concerts.) I am thrilled and excited as you can imagine.

But it took me *ages* to get to this point.

The first step was getting brave enough to send that first email with my CV. I was so excited and sure that I'd get an email by return of 'post', offering me my first concert with them right away. Naïve fool that I was…

About *six months later* I wrote another email, and some weeks after that I managed to get a colleague to introduce me to the orchestra manager during a break in their rehearsal. Once again, I was so pleased with myself for my courage and sure it would lead to work immediately.

Not so. Another few months, and at last, out of the blue, they wrote to me to ask if I could play in a concert the following Saturday. They finished with 'See you at 4pm tomorrow for the first rehearsal'. Yikes. Mad rearranging of my private students and…I was away!

The concert was fabulous, I played like a demon (or an angel, whatever), did one more concert with them…and then didn't hear from them for another three months…

One day I sent the manager this email:

'As I have already mentioned, I have spent the last years playing with the 'X' Orchestra as their concertmaster. In the last few months I have been playing with several other orchestras in order to increase my experience and I have now made the decision to leave my present position in order to be more available to play at a more professional level. The concerts that I have already done with your orchestra have helped me to see that this is what I now want and need in order to grow as a professional musician. I will be playing one more concert with my current orchestra and then will be free to dedicate my time in this new way.

Thank you for your attention and with the hopes of being of the greatest service possible.

Yours etc.'

Too much?

Well, the next *day* he wrote back with the offer of two concerts right away and then I worked with them (with monthly contracts) through March, April, May and June…and now I have the new contract for this next season.

Consider these famous words by William Hutchison Murray:

"Until one is committed, there is hesitancy, the chance to draw back, always ineffectiveness. Concerning all acts of initiative (and creation), there is one elementary truth that ignorance of which kills countless ideas and splendid plans: that the moment one definitely commits oneself, then Providence moves too. All sorts of things occur to help one that would never otherwise have occurred. A whole stream of events issues from the decision, raising in one's favor all manner of unforeseen incidents and meetings and material assistance, which no man could have dreamed would have come his way. Whatever you can do, or dream you can do, begin it. Boldness has genius, power, and magic in it. Begin it now."

So I don't believe in coincidences. I call them 'non-coincidences' now. My new liberating belief is that you create your own luck, and thus your own reality. Not necessarily easily or quickly, as you can see, and it takes inner and outer preparation, but it eventually happens if we have faith and hang in there.

(And think how much we learn along the way!!)

Now, clamoring for attention comes the double whammy:

#5 'I can't afford it/I don't have time.'

These beliefs are incredibly powerful. (I think of them as *'No, no, this belief is really true'* beliefs.) If you are in the grip of them you are probably thinking by now: 'It's alright for her. I've got a job, kids, a mortgage and expenses to pay, responsibilities. There is no way I can find the time or the money to indulge myself and 'follow my bliss.'

Those thoughts all came up for me. They are so *true*, aren't they?

And I wasn't really able to make a final move until I had dealt with the concluding belief that I was being horribly self-indulgent, which translated to 'I don't deserve to do this for myself.'

When I started the whole process of doing inner searching, working with a coach and really digging down to see what I wanted, I felt like the most selfish person on the planet.

But consider these two scenarios:

Scenario #1. A world full of people working at jobs they don't really like, feeling grumpy and stressed and angry, crashing out in front of the TV with alcohol or drug of choice before bed. Sleep, wake up, argue with family, feel impatient and fed up with strangers, lather, rinse, repeat. Maybe a few moments on holidays or at the weekends feeling more relaxed and expansive but dreading the return to 'real' life and another Monday morning.

Scenario #2. A world full of people who love what they do, who are working at a job which they find totally fulfilling to the extent that it doesn't feel like work. Smiling and cheerful with their family, friends and acquaintances, spreading optimism and good cheer. Looking forward to Monday mornings, back to doing what they love to do.

I definitely go with scenario #2 and I hope you do too.

So who are these people in the utopic second world? Well, you, me, the neighbor from downstairs and your colleagues at work…

And who gets to change them? Well, you, me, the neighbor, your colleagues… We can't change others (though we might try). We can only change ourselves. And then, hopefully, through our actions and example, inspire others to do the same.

So, is this really a selfish act, or are you doing it for the greater good?

And as for 'deserving' it. Try asking yourself these questions:

'Am I basically a nice person (especially when I'm in a good mood)?'

'Is there anyone else in the world exactly like me?' (*The answer is 'no', even if you're an identical twin like me.*)

'Would I like to be happier and spread more happiness round me?'

'Am I of more use to the world when I am happy and sharing my gifts and talents or when I am unhappy and keeping myself to myself?'

'Is this not deserving thing even **real** *or is it something I picked up when I was small?'*

'Could it be that we can have what we want just by asking for it and allowing it, that it has **nothing** *to do with being deserving or not?'*

By contemplating these questions I got to a place of believing that I was doing this not only for myself but also for the 'highest good of all concerned'. I could see it as a selfish *and* a selfless act. So then I was able to start moving on the practicalities of not having enough time or money.

You know that road sign 'Proceed with caution!'? Well, that's the advice I would give if these particular limiting beliefs are chiming in strongly with you.

In the next section I get into my ideas about taking action and how 'Proceed with caution!' could look at a practical level. For the moment, suffice it to say that I wouldn't start by messing with my current 'reality' (read: 'Don't chuck in the day job yet.'). But rather, start loosening the hold that these limiting beliefs have on you by taking small, non-risky actions and doing inner work. You will come to see them not as insurmountable but as one more thought that can be worked on and eventually changed.

In the meantime, do your current work as if it really is what you love to do, but with the knowledge inside that it is all part of your master plan. Because you know where you are going and that this is just a stepping stone to get to it.

Take your time and miracles will happen in your thinking which will turn into miracles in your life.

#6 'I don't want to rock the boat.'

Another huge one for me...

'No man (or woman) is an island' and I was terrified of upsetting my family, my friends and my colleagues by making changes in my life which could affect their lives too, directly or indirectly.

When I left my teaching job in order to pursue a performing career, by far the most overwhelming emotion I had to deal with (which quickly swamped the initial excitement) was shame.

'How can I leave all these children without their violin teacher?' 'What will my fellow musicians in the orchestra think? Surely they'd all love to do the same but aren't as lucky as me.' 'These changes are going to affect my husband and children. How can I do this to them?'

Two things helped me to stabilize the boat and avoid capsize.

The first was that I made contingency plans. I spoke to two

other violin teachers and made sure that all the students were covered between the three of us (I kept on a handful of private students.) I made sure I had enough money in savings to tide me over while I made these changes.

And the second was that I spoke from my heart about my own feelings. I didn't tell anyone 'You'll be a lot better off without me in the long run' or try to convince them that it really was for their 'highest good' (after all, how am I to know what that is?) I just explained that this was something I really had to do for myself, that it had been a long time coming and that although I hated to risk upsetting them it felt like I just had no choice but to do this for myself.

And I was surprised and very relieved at how much support and encouragement I got from others. All the criticism and 'What on earth are you thinking of?' comments that I'd been imagining just didn't happen.

I realized that, not only do we underestimate ourselves, we also underestimate others.

'I can change and grow to be a bigger person but others can't. They will stay small and want me to do the same.' Ouch. Experience taught me otherwise.

As for my family, I came to realize that any initial concern or resistance on their part was about not wanting to see me hurt, not about keeping me from what I wanted. (Remember my old mentors?)

My Life Coach (once again) summed things up for me by saying:

'Because they love *you. And the more of you there is, the more there is to love.'*

The next limiting belief I want to consider is related to money but from a particular angle, born of other messages we took on as we were growing up.

#7 'I can't earn a living doing what I love.'

I have to admit, I'm still working on this one, but little by little, as I start to change my mind (my thinking) about this, I am starting to see different results.

Where does this one come from?

Well, we've seen, and still see constantly, so many people who believe that work is hard, a drudge, unpleasant, boring and unrewarding. But they do it because they need the money. So our fun comes from things outside of work and outside of our working hours. The idea of having fun *at* work is a completely foreign concept to many of us.

And to make it even worse, try turning this round the other way. The unconscious thinking goes: 'If I take what I love to do and try to turn it into a job and make money from it, then it will also become hard, a drudge, unpleasant, boring and unrewarding.'

So is it any wonder we resist taking what we love, what we are passionate about, and try to earn our living from it? I'd run a mile if playing the violin became such a nasty experience…come to think of it, I did!

This whole idea was a complete eye-opener for me and explained a lot of my resistance. When I realized that that this kind of thinking was consuming me then I was able to replace it with new thoughts; thoughts about deserving, and sharing my gifts and talents, and from that new standpoint I started to take new actions which led (and are leading) to new results.

Another limiting belief which so many people have and which stops us from even leaving the starting gate is

#8 'I don't know how to do it.'

Do you want the good news or the bad news first? Ok, let's delay gratification a little bit…

The bad news is: *'Well, no, you don't know how to do it, all the steps to take, and from right where you are standing you can't possibly know.'*

And the good news is: *'You don't have to know.'*

A couple of summers ago I went on a canal boat holiday in England with my family. We hired a 55 foot narrow boat, had a half hour lesson on how to drive the thing (how nutty is that?) and we were off…

Now, parts of these canals are just amazing. I expected them to be straight. After all, they are manmade so why not take the straightest line between point A and point B, dig a channel, and have a beautiful, direct 'Roman road' to get to where you are going?

But no. They twist and turn, following the contours of the land, sometimes even backing up on themselves, sometimes going relatively straight and sometimes taking totally unexpected directions.

A bit like life, huh?

And like life, there are some parts where you literally cannot see where you are going next, until you move up ahead a little, turn a corner (often with difficulty, these narrow boats are long and awkward and we were clumsy drivers!) and then see the next part of the journey up ahead. A little bit more revealed.

I used to believe that until I had all the steps worked out I couldn't move ahead. Actually, I couldn't even *look* ahead. I think that's what stopped me from setting goals or making plans.

Until I learnt that the goal or plan is just there to keep you moving in a general direction and that you will learn what you need to do along the way.

Consider EFT founder Gary Craig's remark:

'Dreams don't always come true but they take us in directions.'

What a liberating belief that is. I can now state my dream without five hundred internal voices jumping in with comments, putdowns and questions. I can now ask myself, *'What action can I take to get just around that next bend in the river?'* and then clear anything that might still be holding me back, any limiting beliefs or blocks, by tapping on them or clearing them in other ways .

(More on 'taking action' later on.)

We can become unstoppable by taking short stretches of the river…and even enjoying the view along the way.

(And, by the way, dreams *do* sometimes come true. Just saying.)

There's another thing we often can't see. We are told to *'See yourself as the person you wish to become'*. So this limiting belief for me looked like:

#9 'I'm not an Artist' or 'I'm not a professional violinist.'

(Insert your own dream profession in there.)

Again, a lack of vision, not- as my Life Coach is fond of saying- because we are bad or wrong or stupid, but because we've just had no practice at this.

OK, you were probably asked, when you were little, the classic: 'What do you want to be when you grow up?' If you didn't answer 'A teacher' (because that's the only job you'd ever paid attention to up till then!) you probably said 'An astronaut' or 'A princess' or something equally far out there and aspirational.

Let's face it, you didn't have a clue. Or, at least, I certainly didn't.

So the adult would laugh indulgently and say 'Oh, aren't you sweet (funny/ adorable)?'

No, it wasn't a serious discussion and it certainly wasn't of any practical use for you. You didn't learn that you really could become something quite amazing later on in your life.

But how about if you persisted? 'No, really. I *really* want to be astronaut.' How would that have been received? Ever heard: *'Don't get your hopes up.' 'That's not for the likes of us.' 'You're heading for a big disappointment.'* ?

Once again, although it feels like everyone is just trying to rain on your parade, it's more about safety, protection and misguided love on their part.

And once again you can now start to ask yourself different questions and dredge up different evidence until you convince yourself, 'Well, actually I *am* (or can be) an Artist (etc.)'

(Or even a princess if that still takes your fancy. The wife of Felipe, the present King of Spain, Princess Letizia, was just a normal journalist and now look at her!)

My Life Coach said to me once:

'You can't step up on a stage and expect others to see what you can't see yourself.'

True, but here's some more good news. You will find that as you start to think of yourself in this new way it will take on its own momentum. Once I realized that the only thing I had to change was my own *thinking* about myself I found myself *doing* different things to reinforce this new picture.

What a relief not having to start by changing anyone else or circumstances or by having a different set of skills and abilities in that very moment. No, by changing my thinking I would automatically acquire and develop skills and abilities and other people would start to see me in a new light and therefore reinforce my new self beliefs.

#10 'I don't deserve it' or 'This is so self-indulgent.'

I hope that I've already covered these previously…

Once again, I'm going to quote something my Life Coach, Brad Yates, said to me.

'Not only do you have a right to do this. It is your duty to do this.'

Gosh, it makes me want to jump up, put my hand on my heart and start singing the National Anthem!!

#11 'I can't handle change.'

Uh, well, can I remind you of something, as gently as possible? You handle change every moment of your life. You handled everything that has ever been given to you (or thrown at you) in the past. Sometimes, with grace and ease, and sometimes, kicking and screaming and resisting all the way.

But you did handle it. How do I know? Because if you are reading this book, you are still alive, still breathing. So you *did* handle it.

As an exercise, go back through your life and note what is different from when you were a tiny newborn to how you are now.

You can now walk, talk a language (maybe even 2 or more), dress yourself, feed yourself…(I'm talking generally here so apologies in advance to anyone in special circumstances- though you'll probably find that you are the one with even more highly developed other skills…so, good for you.)

You have probably lived in more than one place in your life.

You have probably changed friends several times during your life. Maybe even 'significant others'.

You have changed your hairstyle, your looks, your way of dressing and speaking.

You are doing different things on a daily basis.

And you have certainly changed your way of thinking.

Do you see? You have made huge changes in your life and you have coped with them all.

And do you see another thing? You have expanded. Literally and figuratively.

So do you see how that is a general trend and how that, for as long as you continue to allow yourself, you will continue to expand? Maybe not literally any more, (that might not be so desirable if you are fully grown!), but definitely as a person, as a soul, mentally and spiritually, and yes, physically developing your skills.

I find this an incredibly exciting notion. *The notion that changing and growing isn't something we have to struggle to do. It is a natural process and if we stop blocking and limiting ourselves it will happen on its own.*

I prefer to look on it as 'managing change' rather than 'handling change'. Putting out an order to the Great Chinese Restaurant in the Sky (more of that later in the chapters on 'taking action'), rather than putting up with whatever comes our way and opposing and fighting against change every step of the way.

I want to finish this chapter with just two more limiting beliefs, two sides of the same coin.

#12 & 13 Heads 'I'll fail' and tails 'I'll…(dear God, no) succeed!!'

I knew all about the fear of failing.

The humiliation of breaking down in a concert, the horror of playing badly in an audition, the shame of being moved from a leading position to a lesser position in an orchestra (second year at Trinity.)

And on a personal level, a failed marriage.

Actually, I can't even see them as failures now. Because of two things.

Firstly, that in most cases (of course there are still some things that need work) I have cleared the deep rooted 'negative' emotions around them and so they no longer bring up kneejerk, uncomfortable, upsetting reactions when I think of them.

And secondly, I realized they taught me lessons, and can see how they have led me to where I am now, so I can view them as ultimately beneficial even though they were so painful at the time.

So those 'failures' –or 'learning moments'- can be seen as 'successes' – or 'winning moments.'

Which brings me onto the ultimate limiting belief of **'I'm afraid I'll succeed.'**

I have to admit, this was a totally new concept for me when I first heard of it.

'What? Of course I want to succeed. What a ridiculous idea. The downside of success? There is no downside.'

And then I started to think about it. And think.

I realized that, in fact, success brings up all the other limiting beliefs and fears. Fears of change, of 'deserving', of seeing yourself differently, of not being good enough, of 'rocking the boat'...

And another fear, too.

I remember one session with my Life Coach when I was complaining about feeling totally stuck, that it was all impossible and that I was never going to make it as a professional.

He started a tapping round with the words:

'Even though this might be possible...'

And I was horrified. I'd been expecting, nay, looking forward to, 'Even though this is all *im*possible...'

And how comforting that would have been. I could have stayed in my safety zone, received sympathy, maybe a little advice to keep maintaining the illusion of moving forward, and I wouldn't have to face that terrifying idea: 'This is going to happen'.

I grunted, he laughed, and continued right on. What a nerve! Took a while to forgive him for that one… (the jerk!)

This is what Marianne Williamson had to say about success in her amazing book 'Return to Love'. (Reproduced here with her permission.)

'Our deepest fear is not that we are inadequate. Our deepest fear is that we are powerful beyond measure. It is our light, not our darkness that most frightens us. We ask ourselves, Who am I to be brilliant, gorgeous, talented, and fabulous? Actually, who are you not to be? You are a child of God. Your playing small does not serve the world. There is nothing enlightened about shrinking so that other people will not feel insecure around you. We are all meant to shine, as children do. We were born to make manifest the glory of God that is within us. It is not just in some of us; it is in everyone and as we let our own light shine, we unconsciously give others permission to do the same. As we are liberated from our own fear, our presence automatically liberates others.'

Do not take 'fear of success' lightly. It's worth delving into and pondering because it can be a huge, invisible barrier.

We are afraid that we won't be able to handle our success. We got so used to being told what to do and how to do it when we were children that we don't even realize that *now* we are, as adults, in charge of our own lives.

Which means that if (when) success comes, we can make our own decisions. We can decide to what extent we want to be seen and heard and who gets to share our time and our resources. We can decide how we divide those up so we can continue to be happy and centered without being pulled in too many directions at once. These are all things we can learn along the way so long as we continue to ask ourselves a couple of good questions:

'Does this make me (and the people closest to me) happy?'
'Is this for my highest good, and for the good of all concerned?'
('Is it ethical, legal etc.?')

Have you ever noticed that we tend to downplay the successes we have already experienced?
'Oh, that. That was nothing. I just got lucky.'
Almost as if we might jinx ourselves for future success by acknowledging too clearly what we already have achieved.

I suggest you write a list – a long list – of all the successes you have ever had in your life.

Partly to boost your confidence and give yourself a warm glow, but also partly so that you can see that you, in the same way as I talked about with change, have already handled success, over and over again.

And remember what I said about 'What we focus on expands'? Focus on the success you have experienced in your life and go for more. You will be doing yourself, and everybody around you, a huge favor.

Now we've looked at 'What's stopping you? and, hopefully, started to dissolve the internal barriers and rethink many beliefs, reasons and excuses that have been holding you back, let's look at the next step, which I have entitled 'Following your heart.'

2.4 Following your heart
- Opening up to the possibility

In the previous chapter I moved through many common beliefs which limit our potential and showed how I changed them to liberating beliefs.

In this next chapter I talk about **you**. About why you deserve to go for what you would really like to do, and about starting to recognize and access your untapped potential.

When I began to think about writing this book the first title I came up with was *'If I can do it (at 50), so can you.'* A little clunky, I admit, but it said what I really feel.

The thing is, I am nothing special.

No, no, no. Strike that. I am *incredibly* special.

How do I arrive at that conclusion? Well, let's go back to the dictionary.

Special. *(Pron: spesh-uhl)*
Adjective:
1. *of a distinct or particular kind of character.*

2. *being a particular one; particular, individual, or certain.*
3. *pertaining or peculiar to a particular person, thing, instance etc. distinctive; unique.*
4. *having a specific or particular function, purpose etc.*
5. *distinguished or different from what is ordinary or usual*
6. *extraordinary; exceptional, as in amount or degree.*
7. *being such in an exceptional degree; particularly valued.*

Depending on where you are with your self-limiting beliefs you're going to be able to apply only a few, many or all of these definitions to yourself.

Maybe 1, 2 and 3 are OK. *You are unique*, with your unique finger print (we all know that), your unique life experiences, your unique thoughts and beliefs and take on life. OK so far? And with your unique gifts and talents. Starting to push my luck?

I have come to believe in #4, *'having a specific or particular function, purpose'.*

It may not be so clear at first because we can be good at so many things. In my case, I was good at teaching. I was told many times that I was patient and fun and inspiring. And it may be that teaching is part of my life purpose. But I remember my coach saying to me one day:

'But it's not what you came for...'

Wow. How transcendental is that? It certainly got me thinking. I think I'd just accepted that I if I was good at something it implied that it was what I was meant to do.

Read these words by Wallace D. Wattles in his classic 'The Science of Growing Rich.' Contemplate them, commit them to memory, think them over and over until you turn them into a belief, because they are wonderfully liberating.

'Generally speaking, you will do best in that business which

will use your strongest faculties, the one for which you are best 'fitted'. But there are limitations to this statement also. No man should regard his vocation as being irrevocably fixed by the tendencies with which he was born.

…you CAN succeed in any vocation, for you can develop any rudimentary talent, and there is no talent of which you have not at least the rudiment.

You will get rich most easily in point of effort, if you do that for which you are best fitted; but you will get rich most satisfactorily if you do that which you WANT to do.

Doing what you want to do is life; and there is no real satisfaction in living if we are compelled to be forever doing something which we do not like to do, and can never do what we want to do. And it is certain that you can do what you want to do; the desire to do it is proof that you have within you the power which can do it.

Desire is a manifestation of power.'

Numbers 5, and 6. 'Distinguished, extraordinary, exceptional.'

The way I can think of myself like this without all the 'How bigheaded am I?' voices crowding in, is by reminding that part of me putting me down… *'but so are we all.'*

It's like learning a new language. You know those first grammar lessons:

'I am, you are, he/she is, we are, you are, they are…' (Je suis, tu es, il/elle est etc.)

Repeat after me:

   I am extraordinary.
   You are extraordinary.
   He/She is extraordinary.
   We are extraordinary.
   You are extraordinary.
   They are extraordinary.

Like learning a language, it gets easier with practice…

Think of a special friend or person you admire. Think of the love and appreciation you have for them. Think of the qualities that make them stand out for you. Are they funny, kind, compassionate, wise, generous, brave…?

Now here's something that I read once: **The qualities that you love and appreciate in them are a reflection of latent qualities inside of you.**

Isn't that amazing? When you say:

'Susie is so kind and affectionate with her children.' - That's the part of you that is kind and affectionate.

'Dave has so many brilliant ideas and insights.' - That's the part of you that is brilliant and insightful.

'Bob is so wise and loving.' - That's the part of you that is wise and loving.

Doesn't this mean that definition #7, *'being such in an exceptional degree; particularly valued.'* is not only possible for you, but downright obvious?

You are whatever you want to be, to an exceptional degree and you are particularly valuable. You may not know how or why yet and you may not be anywhere near reaching your potential (how many people are?) but the possibility is there…

Talking of potential leads us to the next sticky question which we will deal with in the next chapter…

'What are you here to do?'

2.5 Following your heart - 'What are you here to do?'

In the last chapter I talked about the possibility of 'following your bliss' and why *you* deserve that possibility.

In this chapter I discuss what your 'bliss' might look like. I give two exercises- a positive one and a negative one- for starting to discover what it is you really want to do. I talk about another common reason for resisting moving forward and finish the chapter with a discussion on being 'ready'.

Let's now move on to defining what exactly *you* have, what are *your* gifts and talents, what is it that makes you so special...?

(Ouch. Did you hear that nasty little voice popping up again with *'You're nothing special'*? I thought we'd dealt with that. Just know for now that those thoughts that we keep thinking over and over are very tenacious. Do the 'Thank you for sharing' routine and let's continue.)

Now, I have to admit, I was lucky. I was pretty clear about what I wanted to do. Play the violin. But I wasn't at all clear about how that could translate into a career and making money for myself. (For others, no problem, but not for me.)

I found that knowing what I wanted was a slight consolation, but also a source of frustration. I came to believe that I was being thwarted, that some great Universal force was having a laugh at my expense. 'We'll give her this longing but not the resources or the means…hee, hee, hee.'

When I heard the phrase, *'What you want wants you'* I could hardly believe it. No way, what a load of B.S. that is…

But it set me thinking. What if? What *if* what I wanted (to become a professional performer, lead a professional orchestra, blah, blah,blah) really *did* want me? And…heavens…*what if I was the one stopping it?* Impossible?

Or only too possible. I knew enough about past programming.

So then the whole idea of *allowing* came into play, and, probably for the first time, started to make an inkling of sense.

What if I could have everything I wanted if I allowed it?

Well, that would be a dream come true, wouldn't it?

Let's, for the moment, do as my Life Coach says and *'Let that rattle around inside for a bit'*…

For the moment, right where I am, I am obeying these guidelines:

'Don't rule anything out. Let's take steps, see what comes up. Let's pay attention to what feels good and right. What gets my mojo working and feels like self-love?'

These same thoughts can be applied if you are still wondering exactly what it is you 'came here to do'.

Let's start negative!

Because, let's face it, one incredibly powerful way of knowing what you *do* want is by listening inside to what you *don't* want and turning it about.

Really hear your thoughts and conversations along the lines of, 'God, I hate…' 'I can't stand…' '…makes me so angry.'

What makes you angry, impatient, bored, frustrated, tired or depressed?

Try, *'Oh, it drives me mad when people come unprepared.'*

Bingo! *'I want to work with people who are as involved and committed to this as I am and come prepared and ready to do great work.'*

How about: *'I can't stand working in such a small, ugly space'?*

Ta daa! *'My ideal working environment is large and light and airy with beautiful furnishings and decorations.'* Or, *'I'd love to work outside in nature.'*

Defining what you want by knowing what you don't want is a very good use of our inner (and outer) complaining, whining, negative part. I say, bring it on!!

Visit this link for a free PDF to complete this exercise.

www.jennyclift.com/freepurposePDFs

And now we can get positive.

Imagine you are in a newsagent where they sell newspapers, books and magazines on every imaginable subject. Now, walk over to the magazine rack and, at random, take down three to five magazines. Which ones catch your eye? Which subjects do you find interesting, worth spending time reading and learning more about?

When I did this exercise, first introduced to me by the great money coach T. Harv Eker (information about his online program near the end of this book), I 'picked up' a magazine about yoga and meditation, another about violin technique, one about EFT, one about parenting teenagers (hah!) and one about cats.

So there I had five topics that I was interested in. Try it for yourself.

Now, imagine that you worked in one of these fields. Say, as a yoga and meditation instructor. *How does it feel to tell a friend* (a very open, interested friend who is an excellent listener) *about your job, what you do on a daily basis and what plans you have for your work and career?*

Try: 'I'm going to start making videos to help people get the most out of yoga at all levels. I'll try out the exercises with my favorite students…all of whom are wearing the special yoga gear that I've designed and produced with my fantastic business partner.'

How does that feel? Wonderful? Or is there some resistance coming up?

Try these anti-resistance sentence starters:

'If no one else was in any way affected by my doing these things, I would…'

'If money was not an issue, I could…' (and I could even imagine doing this for free…)

'If I didn't feel so stupid and embarrassed even talking about this, I'd…'

'This sounds totally crazy and way out of my league, but it keeps popping back into my head over and over again…' **INNER HUNCH or INTUITION ALERT!! DO NOT DISCOUNT!!**

From these imaginary conversations (which I would strongly advise you to write down- amazing how we forget our brilliant ideas and plans…or is it?) you will start to get ideas and a small spark will be ignited…

Visit this link for a free PDF to complete this exercise.

www.jennyclift.com/freepurposePDFs

Are you still resisting?

One of the blocks that was very big for me was the fear of losing the good friends and colleagues that I had made along the way. Self-help gurus cheerfully tell us that we need to mix with successful people (rich, famous etc) if we ourselves are to become successful (rich, famous).

OK, let's (quickly) get back to the whole thing of potential. If you are starting to see the possibility of being successful (etc) one day, and that the potential is there within you, can you see that *the potential is there in everyone else too*?

You see, we tend to judge other people by their actions whereas we judge ourselves by our intentions.

We tend to forget that other people have as many things swirling around in their heads and hearts as we do. We see *ourselves* doing less than we could be doing and we say, 'Oh, but I would if I could, it's just that...'

But we see *others* doing less than, and we think, 'Oh, they're obviously not interested (or worse.)' Ouch. Is it just me who falls into this kind of thinking? Just because I can't hear what's going on for them. But, at last I have started to see that we *all* have potential.

And that we also each have our own life path to follow, in our own time and in our own way.

Look at your life as a novel . Your story. You are the main character (of course) and there are other people in this story. Now, there will be a few characters who will be there all the way through or in major sections of your story. And, at the other extreme, there will be people who are in just a paragraph, or maybe a chapter or two.

We can understand that in a book. But in real life it is much easier to let people come than go. If we 'lose' people it is as if something is wrong. It says something bad about us or our behavior or the way we are running our lives and it is a source of great suffering. Instead of seeing it as part of the book, part of the story.

Rest assured that the people who are meant to be there until the end of the novel *will be*. And the others? Well, they were just visiting, enriching your life for the time being and are now busy completing their own story. There's no blame or shame, just a bigger picture- Shakespeare's 'stage' and we are all just actors playing our parts.

And now for one last word about being 'ready'…

Do you know how to drive? Yes? And when you started driving, were you really ready to drive? Did you know all the techniques, the rules and regulations, did you have the experience and know everything there was to know to be a superb driver?

Probably not. You weren't ready.

But then suddenly there came a moment when you were *ready*. Ready at least to go for it, to give it a try.

And so you learnt along the way, what needed to be learnt, and now you can drive. (A car at least, try a canal boat!)

It's the same with your dream career. You may not be ready, but one day you will know you are *ready*. And you will, as the slogan goes, 'Just do it.'

Start as slowly as you need…but start. A moving object gains momentum…

In this chapter we used a negative and a positive exercise for discovering exactly what it is you want to do. I also talked about how we often resist moving forward for fear of losing people along the way, and finished the chapter with a discussion on being 'ready'.

In the next chapter we are going to continue our building, starting from the foundations and moving up.

I talk to you about another of the tools –writing - that has been so helpful in my life. I introduce you to two 'Gratitude' exercises that I have used, and use, regularly, and to an exercise for clearing on a deep level, called '70x7'. I then talk about how I use a daily 'log' to help me move forward and do an exercise for creating the best possible upcoming experiences in your life, which I call 'Intentioning'.

> Visit the link below for the 2 free PDFs: 'Finding what you want – Negative' and 'Finding what you want – Positive.'
>
> *www.jennyclift.com/freepurposePDFs*

Part 3
Building a skyscraper — More Tools

In the last chapter I introduced exercises to discover what it is you really want to 'build' and discussed how our fear of 'losing' people along the way can stop us from moving on. I finished the chapter with the idea that you may never be completely ready but that at some point you will recognize that it is time to 'just do it'.

In this chapter I am going to talk about how I've used writing, specifically writing exercises around gratitude and clearing blocks. I will also explain how I keep a daily 'log' to keep me moving and taking action and how I use an exercise which I call 'intentioning' to create the best possible 'next' experience.

Now that we've established the vision, we're going to start building.

Logically enough, we start with the foundations. Even before seeing the outer edifice we've got to dig deep into the ground. And the taller and more impressive the building, the deeper we have to go.

And if we're going to dig we need tools. And techniques with which to use these tools.

Here are some that I have used over the years, apart from EFT. I will present them in the order that I started to use them in my own life, in my own excavations.

3.1 #1 is Writing

All different kinds of writing.

When I was at boarding school I kept a diary. I wrote in pencil, in tiny writing and every entry started: 'Woke up, got up, had breakfast.'

The other day I fished all those little books out and looked through them. Most of them are totally illegible (thank God for small mercies) and they really are incredibly dull. I know that the impulse behind those diaries was the sense that, somehow, if I didn't write a daily log it was as if I didn't exist, as if my life and past was vanishing behind me. It could have something to do with my rotten memory as I have very few memories of childhood. I don't think I was paying attention! Luckily I have an older sister who can tell me lots of stories so I know I *was* there!

As I moved into adulthood I have upheld the writing habit. For many years I have taken notes after my violin lessons and during my practice. Observations, ideas and exercises.

As I got more involved with personal development I started a series of notebooks. I always have one on the go, and they are a lot more interesting than those school diaries. (Now I 'wake up, get up, meditate and make breakfast for the girls'!)

Here are the kinds of things that I put in these notebooks:

3.1. Gratitude exercises:

#1 Lists.

For me, gratitude is a way of keeping connected. Connected to the good things in my life and to Source (God, the Universe etc) and recognizing and appreciating that source. It is a means of keeping the channel open and the flow going.

Remember I mentioned Susan Jeffer's book, 'Feel the fear and do it anyway'?

The gratitude exercise that she explains is *writing a list at the end of every day of at least twenty things for which you are grateful.*

Little things ('The cat sleeping in my violin case while I'm practicing', 'That first mouthful of gin and tonic'), big things ('Email today from the orchestra!!! 33 concerts over the next 4 months! Yay!!!'), people ('Thanks to my Dad for looking after the girls today', 'Friendly guy in the chicken shop', 'Laughing with Blanca in the rehearsal'), possessions ('I love my new resin, it smells so delicious', 'My bed is so comfortable'), my body ('Feeling fit and healthy doing yoga today', 'My hair went so beautifully today, I LOVE my hairdresser').

You name it, it goes on the list.

It was surprisingly difficult at first. I would dry up after about five items. So I found myself seeking things out during the day so I would have something to put on my list. Deliberately looking up at trees when I was walking down the street so I could write later 'The pattern of the leaves against the sky.' Deliberately noticing a smile here or a joke there when with other people.

This exercise is incredibly powerful and really gets you on an upward spiral of optimism and appreciation.

And you know what they say: *'You get more of what you focus on.'* So you really do increase the good in your life. A win-win situation!

> Visit the link below for a free PDF: 'Gratitude List' Template.
>
> *www.jennyclift.com/freegratitudelist*

#2. Writing gratitude 'lines'.

Another gratitude exercise is one that I used a lot when I was building up my teaching practice. The school was on the outskirts of Madrid and I live right in the centre so I had a metro journey of an hour each way. A perfect time for preparing classes or doing other things.

So I would write a page or two of *'Appreciation Statements'*, nonstop, filling my notebooks with repeated phrases. (Back then I used to hope people on the metro wouldn't think I was crazy for writing 'lines' in a book, now it's for tapping (very discreetly) on my face!)

I would start with:

'Thank you for all of my students and for the hundreds of signs of progress, dedication and enjoyment that I receive from them.'

And then I would write:

'I bless (insert student's name) with love.'

And I would write that for each and every one of my students, yup, even when I had sixty under my supervision.

I would then continue by blessing the premises where I

worked, the coffee machine (important), the photocopier, the other members of staff etc.

It took ages, and I was a little obsessive perhaps, but I'm also convinced that it played a huge part in my success at building up that business.

Think of it as simple economics: **'What you're not appreciating you're depreciating.'**

> Visit the link below for a free PDF: 'Gratitude Lines' Template.
>
> *www.jennyclift.com/freegratitudelines*

Another exercise that I used, this one for clearing out stuff (think of it as removing the rubble from the building site), is called

3.2 'Seventy times seven'

A number of years ago I read a book called *'The only diet there is'* by Sondra Ray, following a recommendation by Louise Hay in her book *'You can heal your life.'*

Sondra Ray's book is about self-love and forgiveness. Forgiving the people in your past and forgiving yourself. Using the exercises in this book I started the process of clearing past resentments, hurts, and misunderstandings, a process that I then continued with EFT.

This particular exercise, her '70 x 7', starts with a statement. She recommends starting with:

'I, (your name), completely forgive my mother.'

So I started with that. (This will be my own daughters in ten years' time!)

You write this sentence out seventy times for the next seven days. And at the bottom of each page you leave some space to note down the thoughts that come up as you write.

Like: 'No, I don't. I'm still mad at her for....'

'Why should I forgive her? She doesn't deserve it.'

'I hope this will free me up to stop feeling so guilty about my own parenting.'

'This feels so stupid. What am I doing this for?'

I did this with several different statements and would find that, as the week passed, the objections became fewer, and I would start having more positive, loving thoughts like 'Well, she did what she could.'

And I would end up feeling so much better and realize that this *process was not really about the other person at all but about giving a gift to myself.* I had a huge realization too that the things that I criticized other people for were things that I didn't like in myself.

I started using the affirmation:

'I release the need to criticize myself THROUGH others.'

I did this process with the statement: 'I, Jenny Clift, with God's help, commit to becoming a professional violinist' and cleared so many misconceptions and doubts and fears that week that it was well worth the time invested.

Because you might be saying, 'Jenny, I haven't got the time for this.'

Let me answer that with my one rule (and I'm not very hot on rules.)

'DO MORE THAN NOTHING.'

So, if that means 10 x49 instead of 70 x 7 (do the math!), so be it.

It's the same as I tell my students (or their parents) when they ask how long they should practice the violin;

'Do more than nothing, every single day.'

Because you are trying to create a habit. And you will find that time gets amazingly bendy and you can fit all kinds of things in that you never could before...

3.3 Keeping a daily log

Now we are talking time management, let me share another use for my notebooks.

Here's how I lay them out (at the moment, it varies…):

Gratitude: 1. Really nice chat to Pam last night.
2. Emma making new friends at school.
3. Orange juice this morning.
(or more.)

Today: Meditation   Yes
Yoga   Standing poses
Exercise   T25-Cardio
EFT   B.Y.'s 'Being a channel for genius.'
             7pm. Magtap call.

Appointments, commitments: 3pm Teach Irene.
6pm Rehearsal with the OSC.

Do list: *Email Beare's about selling violin in auction.*
Google Cultural Centres for concerts with Cy.
Call 3.

Write: *Mindmap & outline. 'Meditation'.*
Type up 'Limiting Beliefs'.

Practise: *Wagner for Saturday*
Paganini for class with Clayton

As I complete the tasks I tick them off.

If there is anything I *haven't* done, for whatever reason (not enough time, procrastination etc.) I circle it. That way I can look back and see what still needs doing, what needs to be broken into smaller chunks or whatever might have resolved itself without my 'help'.

On the in-between pages I write notes on things that I am working on, on teleclasses that I listen to online, on things that are bothering me and any other information that I pick up during the day. It could be a list of twitter addresses to use the next time I am publicizing a concert, phone numbers, addresses, a paragraph from a book I am reading or a tapping round I have invented.

Sometimes I write a lot and sometimes not much but I find it very useful to have everything in one place.

3.4 'Intentioning'

This is something that I have been using more and more recently and I find it fascinating to see the results from 'paving the way', which is what this exercise does.

Consider a situation that is coming up for you today and how you would like it to turn out, how you would like to feel, what you would like to happen, and even how you would like the other people involved to act and behave.

I've found this works especially well with a situation which I am worried or concerned about.

Just one caveat: Remember the phrase: 'This, or something even better, for the highest good of all concerned'. Quite apart from not being *able* to manipulate others to do your will, it's not actually *desirable*. (Not from the point of view of your Higher Self anyway, as I'm sure you'll agree!)

Now, write down:

'I intend to…' or *'My intention is to…'*

and complete with your 'best case scenario' for what is coming up with you.

Let me give you an example which happened for me recently.

This is what I wrote in my notebook (names changed to protect identities):

"Friday, June 12th.

I am a super-powerful manifestor!!

In yesterday's rehearsal I was fretting about David, sitting in front of me, and shooting me what I perceived to be critical glances, and feeling irritated with Sara, sitting next to me, who wasn't playing very well and had the music stand in an awkward place.

So I tapped on these two things and then wrote the intention:

'I intend to have a wonderful rehearsal today, sitting next to someone I really feel good with and feeling happy and relaxed.'

First half of the rehearsal- no 'issues' from either and the angle of the music stand was good.

Second half- The woman up ahead has to go…so Sara moves forward, now sitting next to David (hah!) and I get to sit in a line with Saul and Elena and we have a brilliant time!!

How cool is that?"

What I loved the most about this was that the Universe came up with such a simple and elegant solution (no broken bones or hurt feelings!).

And this happens time and time again.

That for me sums up the word 'awesome'!

I have varied over the years with other things but there has always been writing. It is fascinating to read back and see how I have developed and how things have panned out over time…

This chapter introduced some of the different writing exercises that I have used –and still use- to help me build the foundations for creating my 'skyscraper'. These exercises included gratitude lists, gratitude lines and a clearing method called '70x7'. I also explained how I use a daily 'log' and how I use a method I call 'intentioning' to create great upcoming experiences.

Apart from EFT and writing, another tool that I use on a daily basis is meditation. In the next chapter I write about how I started meditating and discuss some of the benefits I have found from meditation. I give some practical tips or guidelines for starting to meditate and finish with my 'Five Stage Meditation'.

In the last chapter I talked about writing and the different writing exercises- from gratitude lists and lines and a clearing exercise called '70x7', to keeping a daily 'log' and using 'intentioning' for paving the way for the best possible upcoming experience.

In this chapter I talk about how I started meditating and what benefits I have enjoyed so far from practicing meditation. I give some tips and guidelines for starting out and close the chapter with a 'Five Stage meditation', a twenty minute meditation that I have developed and now use on a daily basis.

3.5 #2 is Meditation

My Meditation Story

I am a relatively new meditator.
For many years I was drawn to try meditation, spurred on by the many people who talked of its wonderful benefits.

But I was totally and utterly convinced that I would be useless at meditation. No, even worse, completely incapable. My mind was just so chaotic and speedy. How on earth was I going to slow it down and allow myself to become serene and calm?

I remember thinking (once again), 'It's just not me. Apart from my racing mind I'm so superficial. I'm not the kind of person who goes deep inside and connects with their inner stillness.'

Yes, *I had the typical picture of a meditator as someone with a long, flowing beard, sitting in a cave in just a loincloth for years on end with a beatific smile on their face, from time to time bestowing gentle wisdom and loving words and looks…*

No, *really* not how I thought of myself.

But it kept returning, this urge to meditate. I suppose it was an unconscious 'knowing' that it would be beneficial to me in the long run.

So I made up my mind to meditate every day.

I started early one morning before any of my family was up. I sat on the sofa, closed my eyes and tried to focus on just my breathing.

It was hopeless. I couldn't do this for toffee. My mind was off, galloping about like a wild pony. Now I felt even worse. I had known all along that I'd be rubbish at this.

So I decided to tap at the same time: *'Even though I can't meditate, I deeply and completely love and accept myself.'*

As I went through the points, giving voice to the 'I can't do this' 'My mind won't keep still' 'Oh, why can't I concentrate?' Then I realized that I was at least staying with the experience, staying in the 'here and now', and at the same time clearing my blocks and doubts.

Basically I allowed myself to be crap at meditating…which opened up the way to be able to do it.

After a few days like this I decided to investigate meditation, which led to mindfulness and YouTube once again. (I laugh at myself and my former reluctance to computers now. I've certainly made friends with *that* monster!)

There are some absolutely wonderful practitioners out there and I can never get over the amount of free material available. What a gift!

I would email myself links of the ones I particularly enjoyed (Find these links in Part 5, chapter 1, Outside Help, Further Resources link):

Breathing meditations by people like Jeremy Woodall and Linda Hall.

Body scans by Mindah-Lee Kumah, 'The Enthusiastic Buddhist' (a gorgeous young Australian woman).

Meditations for being in the present moment by Lori Granger

and one of my favourites, a 'Guided meditation on Joy' by 'MindfulPeace'.

I also discovered, and was totally blown away by, Paul Santisi's amazing 3D-sound meditations, although they are maybe a little different, more a cross between hypnosis and affirmations.

Although I loved listening quietly to online meditations, and still do so very often, I had a couple of problems with them. The first was that, in a funny way, it felt like I was 'cheating'. A bit like having a story read to me instead of reading it for myself.

And the other was that if I opened up my computer I would find myself an hour later still checking my emails or 'liking' Facebook posts. *Not* quite the point!

So I decided to go it alone. I had listened to several teleclasses and even bought a course about meditation so I had gleaned a few rules and bits of advice (See more information about those courses in the later chapter on 'Inspiration-online courses'.)

By now I had also realized that all my years of doing yoga - with body scans in relaxation pose at the end of a session, as well as concentrating within while doing Asanas - had now paid off. Add to that all the years of violin practice, training myself to focus on different elements in order to improve. Both of these had already given me a good grounding in the art of meditating.

I started to feel some benefits…

3.6 Benefits of Meditation

#1 'Taming' or releasing the inner critic.

As a violinist you have to practice a *lot* so it's very helpful if you enjoy it. I always have, but with one drawback. I used to give myself an incredibly hard time inside my own head. If I made a mistake it wasn't just a question of noting and adjusting. No. My mind would be off; criticizing, prophesying doom and failure and generally beating myself up.

Not quite so unpleasant, but equally distracting, were the thoughts of 'Oh, that was good. Now you're getting it. Maybe, just maybe, you'll get this someday.'

But first by clearing so many things with EFT, and secondly through practicing meditation, I suddenly came to realize I wasn't doing any of that any more.

Wow, what a weight lifted off me.

#2 Giving myself a mental 'time off'.

If #1 was 'giving myself a break' in the sense of not being so hard on myself, #2 is giving myself a break, as in a *rest* from thoughts and the constant chatter and activity in my mind.

This has developed with time. Just the other day I had woken feeling stressed and cross. I sat down to meditate, almost jumped up, impatiently, and then made a deliberate decision to take a time out from my mind.

What a wonderful relief. I felt so much better by the end and was able to go on to have a great day instead of one that had promised to be full of irritation and frustration.

#3 Deliberately training good feelings - both physical and emotional - during meditation.

One day it suddenly occurred to me: 'Ok, if we're breathing all the time, how wonderful would it be to be able to tap into wonderful feelings through the breath?'

Instead of feeling good because of someone or something outside of myself (which, of course, is out of my control), I could train myself to feel great just by concentrating on my breathing.

How cool would that be?

So I used my meditation practice to train good feelings…and it works!

I fully expect more benefits to show up as I continue to meditate and deepen my understanding of it over time.

3.7 Practical Tips for Meditation

Now here are a few tips I have learnt from others and through my own practice. Without in any way pretending to be an instructor, I will share them here, in the hopes that they might be useful if you are not already in the habit of meditating.

#1 Find a place and a time that you can be alone.

It doesn't have to be quiet, (in fact, noting sounds can be a part of the practice,) but you do need to know you won't be disturbed. I get up earlier than the rest of the household, or I tell my family that I need to be undisturbed for fifteen or twenty minutes. They are used to it now and leave me alone.

#2 Set a timer or an alarm or have a watch handy.

Turn the sound down on your timer so you don't get a fright as you come out of the meditation.

If you do the same amount of time each day you will know very quickly, to the minute, when you are coming to the end of your session.

#3 Follow the golden rule: 'Do more than nothing'.

Every day. If that means just two minutes for starters that is absolutely fine. What we're trying to do here is form a habit and train certain reflex responses.

#4 Choose a posture which is comfortable and sustainable, but which is *different* from other activities.

I find lying down or sitting back on the sofa tend to make me sleepy. Keep your back straight. I sit cross legged on a cushion on top of a blanket. If you are on a chair that's fine, but sit at the edge of the chair with your feet flat on the floor, legs uncrossed. I put one hand resting inside the other, palms up and gently rounded. Not a usual position for me.

Once again, it's the Pavlov dog thing. It's like a signal to my body and mind: 'Now we're going to meditate.' They will start to react in a similar way each time you prepare to meditate and it will get easier and easier.

#5 Start by setting an intention.

I've found this to be useful, especially on days when my mind is particularly active. It's a little like a teacher calling the class to order at the beginning of a lesson.

Here's an example:

'I intend to focus on the here and now.
I intend to pay attention to my breathing.
I choose to let myself relax and feel centered and peaceful.
I intend to feel connected.'

Something along those lines to gather yourself together.

#6 Know your mind will wander.

This may be the most important thing to know. It's pretty much inevitable. After all, our minds are designed to think. That's their job.

Some days they will go off a *lot*, hundreds of times in one session. Sometimes not so much.

But the practice is not about having no thoughts nor having a completely clear mind. (Although that's certainly something to aim for).

No, it's about catching yourself wandering off, and that sometimes takes quite a while. Then gently acknowledging the thought and steering yourself back to the task in hand. Like training a puppy. Recognize that it's not going to stay in one place and allow that to be OK.

Above all, welcome your mind back with open arms: 'Hello, you came home! It's so good to see you again!' And then keep right on.

Once, I heard: *'The healing is in the return'*. That suddenly made it all right, in fact, positively *beneficial* to have thoughts come in, so that I could get some more healing as I guided my mind back.

And, once again, as you allow it to happen and stop resisting, you will find that it becomes less of an issue and starts to fade away.

> Visit the link below for a free '21 Day Meditation Plan.'
>
> *www.jennyclift.com/free21daymeditation*

3.8 *Five Stage Meditation*

This is the meditation that I have developed over the last year or so. I would especially like to acknowledge Mindah-Lee Kumah, Christie Marie Sheldon and Dr. Kristin Neff here who inspired me (via their free YouTube videos and their websites) to some of the different techniques I use here.

The stages lead into each other and take about three to five minutes each but you can be as free as you like with the timing. No strict rules here. Just whatever feels good or right.

If you find yourself getting uncomfortable during the meditation, shift your position gently and slowly. As you continue to meditate you will get used to sitting in your posture for longer.

Preparation:

1. Sit in your preferred meditation posture.
2. Gently close your eyes or leave them resting unfocused on one spot.
3. Set your intention to stay here and now for the next minutes.

Stage 1: Breathing

Start by observing your breath. Without changing your breathing pattern, observe the breath flowing in and out. Think of your stomach as a balloon. Feel it expanding on the inhalation, stretching the skin, and relaxing on the exhalation as the air flows out. Start the next breath from that place of relaxation and continue to quiet and calm your body and mind.

Take between 5 and 10 breaths this way.

Keep coming back to your breath if a thought comes in.

Stage 2: Body Scan

1. Now pay attention to your feet and legs. Feel the connection to the floor or the chair. Feel any tightness, discomfort, temperature or other sensations. Feel how the muscles and the bones interplay to form the position you have chosen. Marvel at their flexibility and intricacy.

   Say to yourself: *'Feet grounded'*.

2. Move your attention to your hands. Feel how the hand on top rests gently in the palm of the other. Are your hands warm, cold or neutral? Feel the bones within the skin.

   Can you feel any sensations of tingling, the energy in your hands and fingers? Imagine holding a ball of golden energy in your hands.

   Say to yourself: *'Hands rounded'*.

3. Now observe your spine within your back. Hold it straight, imagining each vertebra stacked one on top of the other right

from the base of your spine to the base of your neck. Centre yourself with your weight right over your pelvis. Imagine your spine stretching up like a plant towards the sun.

Say to yourself: *'Back tall'*.

4. Relax your shoulders. Allow them to drop a little and feel the energy flowing down your arms into your hands, relaxing them as it goes.

Say to yourself: *'Shoulders fall'*.

5. Slightly lower your chin and feel how that opens the vertebrae in the back of your neck.

Say to yourself: *'Neck open'*.

6. Allow yourself to smile just a tiny bit. Like revisiting a memory of happiness. Turn the corners of your mouth turn up a little and feel the muscles of your cheekbones slightly contracting. Feel which muscles are stretching and which are contracting as you hold this smile. Allow yourself to relax into the good feelings which accompany this smile.

Say to yourself: *'Mouth smile'*.

7. Now feel into your eyes. Allow them to soften and relax.

Say to yourself: *'Eyes soft'*.

Now move slowly and gently back down your body saying inwardly:
'Eyes soft.

Mouth smile.
Neck open.
Shoulders fall.
Back tall.
Hands rounded.
Feet grounded.'

Feel the sensations in your body as you say the words to yourself.

Go up and down the body one or more times saying the cues.

Stage 3: Noting sounds and thoughts or emotions.

Listen to the sound of your breathing. Listen as the air flows in and out.

Next listen to the sounds in the room where you are. The hum of the computer, a clock ticking, any small rustles or movements. Make a short mental note of each sound. 'Computer humming'. 'Clock ticking'. etc.

If there is silence note the silence.

Now listen to any sounds outside the room or building. Make a mental note. 'People talking', 'Car accelerating', 'Dog barking'. Once you have noted the sound move to the next one, allowing yourself to be carried in the flow of sound. Don't strain. Just allow the sounds to come to you.

Now 'listen' to the thoughts or emotions that come into your head. Again, make a short mental note: 'Planning'. 'Thoughts of my children'. 'Thoughts of what happened yesterday'. Or 'Nostalgia', 'Excitement', 'Boredom'.

Allow them to come in, name them, and allow them to go again. If you get carried away make a mental note of that: *'Carried away'* and come back to noticing the thoughts and feelings again.

Stage 4: Connecting up and down.

Imagine a space in the sky about 300 feet up, about 27 stories of a building. Slightly tilt your head back and 'see', right there, a door in the clouds. Open the door and allow a golden beam of energy to shine through, almost a solid column of golden light. This energy is straight from the Source of love, kindness, goodness, fun, joy, beauty, peace, calm, inspiration and happiness. Allow yourself to be washed in this beam of light. Feel it moving down your body, filling you with this light, then straight through the floor, down into the earth, down until it reaches the centre of the earth. Here there is a core of pure love. Allow this to bounce back right up into your body. Feel the sensations, both physical and emotional, that this produces in you.

Stage 5: Loving kindness.

Let this loving energy radiate out from your body in a globe about 10 feet all around you.
　Say to yourself:
　'May I be happy.
　May I be free from suffering.
　May I feel calm, loving and connected, within and without.'

　Now expand the light globe to encircle the building in which you are. Say to yourself:
　'May all beings in this space be happy.
　May they all be free from suffering.
　May they feel calm, loving and connected, within and without.'

　Let the light expand to the size of the town, city or place where you are. Once again:

'May all beings in this town be happy.
May they all be free from suffering.
May they feel calm, loving and connected, within and without.'

Now grow your light globe to fill the state where you are and say:
'May all beings in this state be happy.
May they all be free from suffering.
May they feel calm, loving and connected, within and without.'

Now the country where you are located:
'May all beings in this country be happy.
May they all be free from suffering.
May they feel calm, loving and connected, within and without.'

Now encircle the whole planet in your light and say:
'May all beings on this earth be happy.
May they all be free from suffering.
May they feel calm, loving and connected, within and without.'

Gently come back to your breath. Take three deep breaths in and out. Now gently open your eyes. Stretch a little. Slowly and quietly allow yourself to come back to the room where you are and to go about your day.

Meditation is a gift that you give to yourself.

I hope that the tips and steps that I have outlined in this chapter will encourage you to form (or enhance) your own practice…

> Visit the link below for a free 21 Day Meditation Practice Plan.
>
> www.jennyclift.com/free21daymeditation

Now we are busy digging the foundations for our building with the help of these different tools we're going to consider the next, very important step.

Making a blueprint…

Part 4
Building a skyscraper – Plan and Act

In the last chapters I talked about the different tools that I use apart from EFT- specifically writing exercises and meditation.

In this chapter we are going on to create a 'blueprint'; using a technique called 'mindmapping' we will discover our longterm goals, and then make yearly, weekly and daily plans filled with actions which will bring us nearer to achieving those goals.

🎼 4.1 The Blueprint

Obviously when constructing any kind of building, but especially a sky-scraper, it is necessary to have a blueprint. Something down on paper with a clear image of the finished product, with details and instructions which enable it, eventually, to be created.

This is where goal setting and planning come in.

Now, I have to be very honest here.

This is the third time I have attempted to write this chapter. Goal setting and planning do not come easily to me. As I've mentioned before, I was never trained in this and it brings up a *whole* lot of resistance.

Which is good. I suppose.

In fact, that is my first reason for setting a goal and making a plan.

To bring up all the blocks; all those fears, all those voices in your head telling you why this is impossible. Because then we can get on clearing them as part of our inner foundation work.

This resistance may show up as 'laziness', procrastination or tiredness. It could be other things to do, or losing vital pieces of information. Or it could manifest as feelings such as irritation, low self-worth, depression, sadness and general malaise.

These last few days I've been through all of the above.

Two days ago I got up early and after sending my daughters off to school I actually went back to bed. I was exhausted! And I can tell you, I am never exhausted.

I lay there thinking, 'What is going on here, Jenny?' and I realized that I had huge resistance to even just thinking about all of this.

So I tapped a little. 'Even though I *really* don't want to write this chapter...I love and accept myself.'

And then I was able to get up and get going.

I had a notebook. A big A4 sized, bright yellow exercise book, which I had used a few years ago when I did an online course about planning, with the speaker, writer and coach Derek Rydall. (Information about his courses in Part 5, chapter 1 on Outside Help.) He had introduced me to the tried and trusted system of writing a long term goal and then working backwards, and had coached me through the work of writing out all the activities that I would include on that plan.

I *knew* I had the book. It had been sitting on the table under my music stand for about a year. That was what I would use for inspiration and information to help me to complete this chapter.

But I couldn't find it...

It had vanished. Kaput. Gone up in smoke.

I searched my shelves, my drawers, my filing cabinet. I asked the family if anyone had seen it. And I got extremely cross and frustrated.

Luckily, a concert got in the way.

Difficult repertoire for the first concert of the season with my new orchestra, playing in front of no less a dignitary than Queen Sofía of Spain. No way could I go under-rehearsed to this one.

The perfect excuse, nay reason, to stop writing and focus on my violin.

So I gave myself a day off. I spent that time practicing and performing, letting things settle and focusing on feeling very grateful for what I have. And - the concert was fabulous!

Last night I suddenly 'knew' where to find the notebook. And sure enough, there it was, with some papers about my website, sitting smugly, waiting for me to be ready to find it.

Which I now was. The time off had allowed me to clarify some of my ideas, process the feelings and feel ready to tackle this subject.

So here are some

'Blueprint tips or guidelines':

Tip #1, as we've seen, is 'Expect resistance'.

Another rule for having a clear goal is so that you have a general direction in which to move. It's like setting your GPS. You know where you are now and you know your final destination. Which, as you start moving, allows the disembodied voice to start giving you the directions.

Right now you don't have all the instructions and that's not necessary. But she won't even start talking if you haven't put in where you want to end up.

Tip #2, then, is 'Set your GPS'.

And as you begin to drive (take action) you will be able to do so recognizing that there is a reason for each separate action. You will be acting *on purpose*-in every sense of the words.

4.2 Now for making your blueprint

This will take a while, maybe two or three hours (or more), which can be scheduled over the next few days so that 'overwhelm' doesn't set in.

Find a quiet place where you can be alone to dedicate yourself to the process. YOU ARE WORTH IT!

We're going to start with a three year long-term goal and from there, work backwards.

The question to ask yourself is:

'In order to achieve X in three years, what kind of things will I need to be doing in one year's time?'

After that we break down that first year into trimesters, once again working backwards.

'What will I need to be doing in nine months, in six months, in three months, and finally, right now?'

For determining the big three year goal you may need to do some brainstorming in order to clarify your ideas and really start to find out just what it is you are going for.

You can write a list of ideas, or, even better, use a mindmap.

Even though I'm sure you've seen, and probably used, mindmaps, I will briefly explain here how to go about creating one. I've been using them to write this book, on the advice of Chandler Bolt in my Self-Publishing School course (see info later in 'Online courses), and this is how they've worked for me.

4.3 Brainstorming one year goals using a mindmap

Step 1

Take a blank piece of paper, at least A4 size, have paper and sellotape handy in case it needs to grow.

Set a timer for fifteen minutes. Stick with your map for the whole time.

Step 2

In the center of the paper write **'MY 3 YEAR GOALS'** and draw a circle round the words.

MY 3 YEAR GOALS

Now start drawing lines off the circle as ideas start occurring to you.

For example:

MY 3 YEAR GOALS

- Inner Work
  - 15 Mins Daily Meditation
  - EFT To Clear LBs
  - Resistance
    - Journaling
    - What will my family think?
- Eventually leading
  - Networking
    - Facebook
    - Contacts
- Happy and peaceful home life
- Freelancing
- Play in a professional orchestra
  - Improve technical level
    - Clayton Halsop DVDs
      - Paganini
      - Kreutzer
    - New Teacher?
      - Google
  - Audition excerpts & pieces
  - Auditions
    - Where?
      - Ask other musicians
    - Tap on fears around auditions

Stay with this for the whole time and, when the alarm rings you can stop or continue if you still have more to write.

Visit the link below for your free Mindmap template.

www.jennyclift.com/freemindmap

4.4 Turning your mindmap into a one year plan

Step 1

From this mindmap you will discover that you have certain areas which need to be worked on in order to get anywhere close to that 'crazy' dream.

From my example I have these categories:
    Improve technical skills (on the violin).
    Get experience.
    Auditions.
    Contacts and networking.
    Inner work.

Write down your 3-5 categories where your efforts will be concentrated.

Step 2

Now take another piece of paper. I stuck three bits of A4

together lengthways but you can be more classy than that if you want!

Write at the top (changing the year as appropriate, of course.):

ONE YEAR PLAN (2015/2016).

Divide your long paper into six columns. The first and last can be slightly narrower (see below).
The first column is entitled 'Areas to take action in.' The last is 'One year' and the middle ones are divided into trimesters, starting now.

Here's an example:

ONE YEAR PLAN (2015/2016)

Areas	Oct/Nov/ Dec 2015	Jan/Feb/ Mar 2016	Apr/May/ June 2016	July/Aug/ Sept 2016	1 Yr
Inner work Tech. skills Experience Auditions Contacts					

Step 3

Starting at the far right of the page, in the final column, decide where you intend to be and what you intend to be doing in each area in order to be *well on your way* to achieving your big goal.

So you may write:

Inner Work			Self confidence performing. Feeling cool, calm and connected. Meditating regularly as well as daily tapping.
Technical Skills			Vast improvement in my technique and musicality. With new teacher.
Experience			Freelancing regularly with other orchestras.
Auditions			Audition preparation (on and off violin). Do an audition.
Contacts			Business cards. Set up website. Connect with musicians on FB.

Step 4

We are now going to start completing the middle four columns, our four trimesters of the year.

Working backwards complete the chart with 'likely actions.'

	Oct/Nov/ Dec 2015	Jan/Feb/ Mar 2016	Apr/May/ June 2016	July/Aug/ Sept 2016	1 Yr
Inner Work	Start meditating 15 mins daily. Check out EFT. List my limiting beliefs.	Take an online course in meditating.	Find a coach (EFT?) Have a session. Meditating daily.	EFT and daily meditation. Clearing limiting beliefs.	

	Oct/Nov/ Dec 2015	Jan/Feb/ Mar 2016	Apr/May/ June 2016	July/Aug/ Sept 2016	1 Yr
Technical skills	Check out Clayton Haslop DVDs. Plan scales and studies. Kreutzer 1st half.	*Kreutzer 2nd half. Contact Clayton for a Skype class.*	*Paganini studies. Start classes with Clayton.*		
Experience	*Write a CV. Research possible orchestras. Contact.*			*Freelance work with different orchestras.*	
Auditions	*Prepare audition excerpts. Choose Mozart concerto.*	*Audition excerpts to speed. Mozart 1st mov.*	*Apply for auditions. Work on Audition stuff.*	*Do at least one audition.*	
Contacts	Business cards done. Website-do it myself or find a website builder? Research. Research agents.	*Start building website. Make a FB page. Join violin groups.*	*Complete website. www. jenniferclift .com*		

You will find that there are more actions nearer to now and that there are spaces in your plan.

Which is absolutely fine. You are going to update this plan on a regular basis as you start to take action and get feedback on that action.

For now, this is about giving yourself ideas for actions which are directed towards your purpose.

Visit the link below for your free One Year Plan template.

www.jennyclift.com/free1yearplan

4.5 Turning your 'One Year Plan' into a workable plan of action:

Step 1

Take the *first* trimester and on three separate pages - consider getting your own 'yellow notebook' or ringbinder to keep everything together - write:

DAILY ACTIVITIES.

WEEKLY ACTIVITIES.

MONTHLY ACTIVITIES.

Here's an example -assuming you are working around a 'day job' and have limited time available for this. (More about when and how to quit the day job later in the chapter on 'taking action'…):

DAILY ACTIVITIES

6.30 a.m.	Meditation. EFT. Exercise-'Top to toe' and yoga.
7.45 a.m.	Girls up. Breakfast. Take them to school.
9 a.m.	Work.
Lunch hour	30 mins Google orchestra auditions etc.
5.30 p.m.	With the girls. Homework etc. Make dinner. Dinner. Family time.
8 p.m.	Practise-tech. skills and orchestra repertoire.
9.30 p.m.	Work on contacts. Check and send emails.

Of course you will be adjusting the timetable to fit your needs and possibilities.

The point is to dedicate a part of each day to moving towards your goal.

In your **'WEEKLY ACTIVITIES'** you will include things like:

'Violin lesson.'
'Listen to an inspiring teleclass.'
'Contact three concert venues.'

And in the **'MONTHLY ACTIVITIES'**:

'Session with my coach.'
'Read 1 book on personal development or technical skills.'
'Concert.'

Step 2

And finally, use your plans and ideas to start taking regular action.

Some ideas about how in the next chapter…

> Visit the link below for your free Daily, Weekly and Monthly Activities Templates.
>
> *www.jennyclift.com/freeactivities*

4.6 *Get Building*

In the last chapter we created a 'blueprint' which included our long-term goals and yearly, monthly, weekly and daily plans with actions to help you move forward to those goals.

In this chapter I am going to talk about taking action. What it is really for and how to feel less stressed about the whole action thing. I will talk about the big question which came up for me and comes up for many people and how to solve it. Then I discuss taking daily actions and what to do if you don't take an action. And finally the last piece to this whole puzzle, letting go.

> *'The very best thing you can do for the whole world is to make the most of yourself.'*
> — Wallace. D. Wattles

It's time to take action.

How does that make you feel? Fired up and raring to go, or like digging in your heels, reaching for a drink or changing the subject?

Although I am naturally an active person and can make myself do things, whether by habit, self-discipline or sheer will power (until the 'won't power' kicks in too strongly) I have found that being busy and active doesn't always feel the same.

Sometimes it can make you feel great and fulfilled and excited, and sometimes stressed out and worried, the proverbial hamster on its wheel.

I used to feel a lot like that hamster. I would be anxious that if I didn't get moving I would somehow miss all my opportunities, and there wouldn't be anything left for me, I would run out of time and felt that somehow I had to be proving myself over and over again: *'Here, look Universe, I'm serious about this.'*

It didn't feel very good but I didn't know how else to go about it and the alternative-doing nothing- felt much worse. So,

What is action really for?

Recently I have had a radical change in my way of thinking and of viewing action. This enables me to decide what actions to take, when and how to do them and feel good about them.

It's a very simple, but very profound, change of mindset. Here it is:

Once I have decided in my thoughts what it is I want, then anything that I do, any actions that I take, are about preparing to receive *that thing or circumstances.*

A great metaphor for this is that of a pregnant woman.

Imagine a woman who has wanted a child for many years. At last she discovers she is pregnant and is overjoyed. Delighted and grateful that this amazing thing that she has been longing for for such a long time is finally going to come true for her.

So now, does she just sit around for nine months and then out it pops?

No, of course not. She starts preparing.

She goes to childbirth classes and learns all the breathing techniques for labor. She prepares the baby's room; buys a crib, a changing table, little tiny clothes and all the other equipment she's going to need. She takes care of her body, eating healthily and exercising appropriately. She starts to tell her 'nearest and dearest' and shares her excitement with them.

And she dreams. Imagining how her baby will be when it is born. Imagining how it will be to be a mother. Imagining the changes up ahead, sometimes with a tinge of apprehension (or worse!) and sometimes with a sense that she'll handle what is to come, whatever that might be.

So when the baby arrives she has done her preparation, she is ready - inwardly and outwardly - to receive this 'gift' and continue on to the next stage of her life.

And that is how to look at action.

When you write your action steps to take over the next few days, weeks, months, even years, have this question uppermost in your mind:

'What can I do (today, this week etc.) to prepare myself to receive what I have asked for?

The answer might come back:

'Get information about X.'
'Take a course in Y.'
'Clear my fears or resistance around Z.'
'Contact this person who might be able to help me.'
'Write a gratitude list of what I already have.'

There are obviously an infinite number of things you can do. Some of which will be outer actions and some, inner actions.

I have found that when I am resisting taking outer action, when I am procrastinating, it is because more inner clearing and preparation needs to be done first. This goes back to what I mentioned before about clearing out the rubble so that the building can start to be constructed.

Either way, whether you are preparing for outer action or actually taking it, you can rest easy at night knowing that this will happen, this is happening and that *you are making it happen.*

What an empowering state to be in.

When do I quit my job?

A question that plagued me as it cropped up time and time again was *'When do I leave my present job?'*

The same job that is driving me mad, taking up time I could be using to do more interesting and fulfilling things, but that is also the one paying the bills and to which I committed years back.

Obviously everybody's situation is different.

You may be totally ready, on all levels, to chuck it in right away, but the chances are, there is still more to be done right where you are before you move on.

It is still useful for you. AS A MEANS OF GETTING WHERE YOU WANT TO GO.

First of all let's get one thing very clear, with the immortal words of Wallace D. Wattles in his incredible book 'The Science of Getting Rich':

'If you have a strong desire to engage in any particular line of work, you should select that work as the ultimate end at which you aim.

You can do what you want to do, and it is your right and privilege to follow the business or avocation which will be most congenial and pleasant.'

Wow. Your 'right and privilege.' Isn't that the best news ever?

He goes on to say:

'You are not obliged to do what you do not like to do, and should not do it except *as a means to bring you to the doing of the thing you want to do.'*

Now that's worth a second read as, chances are, this is going right against your social conditioning and past programming.

His advice continues:

'If you feel that you are not in the right vocation, do not act too hastily in trying to get into another one. The best way, generally, to change business or environment is by growth.'

By this I understand what I mentioned in the section on limiting beliefs when I talked about 'Showing Up'; being fully present, giving one hundred percent, being professional and responsible and *really there* in whatever activity you are undertaking.

The idea is to grow yourself.

Grow until you have filled your position and then become too large for that position. Until you need a larger place because you are ready to provide more.

This is where the expression *'Nature abhors a vacuum'* comes into play.

Look on yourself as a vessel. Once you have grown too large to hold what you contain now, then nature will see to it that you are sent something new to fill the vacuum.

Which is why it is so important to have a distinct vision, an unambiguous idea of what you want, what you are going, *on purpose*, towards. What *you* desire to fill that vacuum.

Here's the last inspirational quote from our friend Wallace:

'The man who is certain to advance is the one who is too big for his place, and who has a clear concept of what he wants to

be; who knows that he can become what he wants to be and who is determined to BE what he wants to be.'

Small (and big) steps and daily actions.

So, using your notebook and your plan, you can now start taking daily action. Actions which include both inner and outer tasks.
Sometimes the steps will be small, sometimes huge.
Sometimes it will feel like you are surging ahead and sometimes you will feel stuck.
That is all part of the process. Stick with it.

What if I don't do an action?

Keep writing down actions to do each day and tick them off as you complete them.
If you do not complete one, don't worry. Circle it so you know it has to be done the next day.
If you find yourself putting off a particular action several days running, that may be a sign that *either* you need to do some inner clearing around that issue, *or* that the task needs to be broken up into smaller chunks.
Sometimes (fingers crossed) you will find that the Universe just takes care of it without any intervention from you. Or maybe you will decide to go another route.
But remember to keep on doing the inner work so you're not just avoiding the 'hard' stuff.

Whatever happens, **'Don't 'should' on yourself!'** as my coach likes to say.
Above all, be kind to yourself. Self-compassion is so much more beneficial than being hard on yourself.
Unfortunately we all have much more training and practice

in beating ourselves up. But, in fact, that's just another clever way of slowing our progress down.

The fact is *it takes time to come back from feeling miserable and useless.* From now on, start to catch those habitual self-castigating thoughts, thank them for trying to keep you stuck in your safety zone, and then - keep right on at it.

I like to remind myself that if I'm feeling scared or uncomfortable or downright obstinate, it's a *good* sign. It means that I am expanding my comfort zone, growing as a person, making that space larger and so creating a vacuum.

Sometimes it's easier than others. Sometimes I need a good night's sleep or support and help from outside (more on that in the next chapter.)

But I have got better at this with practice and you will too.

'Let go...'

There is another piece in this whole puzzle which is almost like the opposite of action.

It's the whole idea of *'Let go and let God'* (or the Universe, Source, quantum physics...whatever works for you.)

It's that well-known syndrome of the couple who have been trying to have a baby for years, going increasingly miserably down every route imaginable...infertility treatments, IVF, you name it...

So one day they decide to adopt a baby.

And not just decide, but actually take the steps, go the whole way, accepting that this is also a possible solution to making their dream come true.

Then, bam! The next month the woman falls pregnant.

How maddening is that?

I've always found it really hard to get to that place and it's not something you can do to order. That place of relaxing and letting go and accepting that this…*or something even better for the highest good of all concerned*…will happen without me having to *make* it happen.

The *very day* that I received the first email from the new orchestra asking me to play in a concert with them (after almost a year of waiting, and getting increasingly despairing) I had tapped in the morning with the words:

'Even though I may *never* play with a professional orchestra, I choose to love and accept myself.'

And I really meant it, coming to the conclusion that if this wasn't going to happen it was because something else was meant for me and that I was OK with that.

So I have got a little, actually a *lot*, better at trusting and having faith.

Recognizing that if I just keep on taking small or large actions to prepare for receiving, then when and how it will arrive is not my concern. But knowing that it *will* arrive… or, if it doesn't, something even better will be waiting for me.

Recognizing that I have planted a seed. That I am tending to that seed by watering it on a daily basis and nurturing the soil. And, in the meantime, under the ground, out of my sight, it is also doing its bit. In its own right time, one day a shoot will appear.

And after that it gets much easier when you can actually see things happening…

In this chapter I discussed taking action and talked about what action is really for. I talked about the dilemma of 'to quit or not to quit' your job. I went into taking daily actions and what to do if you don't take an action. And then finally the last piece to this whole puzzle, letting go.

In the next chapter I sum up the whole process using an analogy that I call 'The Chinese takeaway restaurant.'

4.7 The Chinese Takeaway Restaurant

Summarizing the steps that we take and the mental attitudes required to create and achieve our vision can be done with the analogy of the Chinese Takeaway Restaurant.

Imagine we are going to order a meal for takeout. Not just any meal. But a special one from an amazing restaurant, the best in town. We have friends over for the evening and we're planning on having a great time.

So what steps need to be taken? And especially, what frame of mind are we in as we take those steps?

#1 We decide what we want.

We look at a menu and choose all the different dishes we fancy.
Deciding between Peking Duck or Sweet and Sour Pork. Dumplings or spring rolls. Fried rice or plain boiled rice.

And when we are discussing the food we use the words: 'I'm going to have...' or even, 'I'm having...'

Our mouths are already watering, imagining this delicious food, savoring the delicacies even before we see, smell, touch or taste them.

We are creating them in our imagination and picturing them in detail.

#2 We phone the restaurant to place our order.

Clearly and precisely.

We don't just say, 'Rice and chicken, please.'

No, we give exact instructions about what we want, even down to the drinks and dessert and the extra soya sauce on the side.

#3. We wait.

But not anxiously. There is no thought of 'Oh, I can't see it yet. What's happening? Maybe they're not bringing it.'

So we don't phone the restaurant every few minutes full of doubts and worries asking: 'Is there a problem? Isn't it going to come?'

And we don't ring again and again, placing the same order over and over, just to ensure that we'll definitely receive what we want.

No, we know it will take a little while even if they haven't said exactly how long. After all, it's got to be prepared and cooked and then delivered.

And so we relax and turn our minds to other things. From time to time revisiting the thought of how delicious this meal is going to be. We feel happy and appreciative knowing that the food is on its way.

#4 **We get prepared to receive our meal.**

We get out the money we'll need to pay for the food and to add a generous tip to the delivery person.
    We lay the table with beautiful linen, plates, bowls and chopsticks. Maybe add some candles as tonight's a special occasion.

#5 **We open the door and receive our food.**

The doorbell rings. Hurray, it's here at last.
    We jump up and open the door. They've brought exactly what we asked for and we sit down and enjoy our meal.

    These exact same steps, and the mindset that accompanies them, are what brings us what we desire in any area of our life.

AS WE SAY IN SPAIN: *¡QUE APROVECHE!*

    In the next chapter I talk about the help and inspiration I have received from outside sources and people and how you can find inspiration for yourself.

Part 5
Don't do this alone

5.1 Outside Help – Get Inspired

This summer I went with my daughters to visit my older sister who lives in Greenwich in Connecticut. We went into New York several times and did all the usual tourist things. We also spent a full day in the American Museum of Natural History in Manhattan.

Apart from seeing wonderful dioramas of North American animals (and my girls were very happy to discover that they aren't real dried and stuffed animals but just big soft toys) we watched a 3D movie in the theatre there, entitled 'Dark Universe'. It was mind-boggling and mind-expanding, talking about 'new frontiers for exploration.'

It set me off once again on the thought of how the journey within ourselves is equally fascinating and mind-expanding. And how inside each one of us there are also always 'new frontiers for exploration'.

I found I could do a lot of delving inside on my own but also needed the inspiration, the new ideas and the different thinking of other people and outside sources.

I have discovered so much information online which has led to me meeting so many new people, both through the computer and in the flesh.

Sources of Inspiration

Here are some of the sources I have found most useful:

#1 YouTube

As I said, I can never get over the variety and sheer quantity, not to mention quality, of the videos people put up on YouTube…all for free.

Type in 'meditations' and you will come up with hundreds of them. That will lead you to mindfulness and Buddhism (I love Tara Brach) and on to Self-Compassion (Dr Kristin Neff's TED talk is a must see). And on and on…

> Visit the link below to find out more about them and their work.
>
> *www.jennyclift.com/freeresources*

2 Online Teleseminars

These are freebie events putting together several speakers focusing on a particular topic. They give away so much knowledge and information and it is just fascinating to hear so many different ideas and takes around a particular subject.

These can lead to…

#3 Online Courses

I have taken courses on many different subjects and have learnt so much from them. These subjects include EFT, creativity, meditation, planning and goalsetting, money, life, stage presence, video making, motivation and success, parenting and writing, self-publishing and marketing.

> Visit the link below to for a free Further Resources PDF.
>
> *www.jennyclift.com/freeresources*

#4 Workshops

These are always advertised as life-changing, and, really, how can they *not* be? I would say they are turbo life-changers.

Quite apart from meeting your teacher in person, you meet so many other fantastic people at these events.

I have only been to three workshops in my life. For the first one I travelled across the Atlantic to San Francisco for one of Brad Yates' workshops and had an incredible weekend. I even got to play the violin during one of the sessions-great therapy for my fear back then of being seen and heard.

I still have one with Rachel Jayne Groover in hand, and one day I will get to one of T.Harv Eker's workshops as well as others I can't even begin to imagine.

> Visit the link below to find out more about them and their work.
>
> *www.jennyclift.com/freeresources*

#5 Books

When I get keen on a topic I love to buy books about it.

I have mentioned other books while writing this one. And of course I have read many more that have inspired and helped me.

Here are some of my absolute favourite (at the time of writing).

'Self- Compassion'	by Kristin Neff, PHD.
'Secrets of a Millionaire Mind'	by T. Harv Eker.
'The Keys to Success'	by Brad Yates. (Ebook.)
'Illusions'	by Richard Bach.
'The Power of Now'	by Eckhart Tolle.
'Dare to be Yourself'	by Alan Cohen.

> Visit this link: for information about them all.
>
> *www.jennyclift.com/freeresources*

You will discover ones that do the same for you, depending on where you are on this journey and what 'speaks' to you right now.

And a fun and easy one:

#6 Inspirational Quotes

If you want to feel uplifted and/or challenged about a particular topic in just a few seconds, google 'Quotes on…' and you will come up with amazing, thought-provoking ideas in an instant. A lot of them with gorgeous images too…

As I said, through all these sources I have gone on to meet many, many incredible people.

Through joining groups on Facebook I have made accountability partners and friends and people who have helped and supported me in so many different ways.

I was terrified of joining Facebook at first and still find myself getting a little overwhelmed by it at times, but it is such an incredible way of meeting other people who are interested in the same kind of things as you.

I belong to violin groups, EFT groups and authors' and self-publishing groups. My mind and, let's be honest, my *heart* are expanded on a daily basis.

So REACH OUT!

Allow yourself to be inspired. *Show up and show willing and you will receive so much.*

And the best thing of all is this; *in the process you will discover just how much you are able to give and be of service.*

I guarantee, it makes you feel *fabulous*!

Contemplate these beautiful words from the late American TV presenter Fred Rogers:

'If only you could sense how important you are to the lives of those you meet; how important you can be to people you may never even dream of.

There is something of yourself that you leave at every meeting with another person.'

Never a truer word was spoken.

In this chapter I have talked about the different sources of inspiration and help that I have discovered along the way. Sources such as YouTube, online seminars and courses, workshops, books and quotes, all provided by incredible people.

> Visit the link below for information about them and how to access their work.
>
> *www.jennyclift.com/freeresources*

These people have been part of this amazing journey, but I couldn't have done it all (or at least, as I started with in my dedication, it would have been very different) without my Life Coach.

So my final chapter is about what to look for in the 'perfect' life coach and how to go about finding one for yourself…

5.2 The 'Perfect' Life Coach

'Our chief want is someone who will inspire us to be what we know we could be.'
— Ralph Waldo Emerson

I got lucky with my coach, Brad Yates. Totally ignorant of the EFT world, I went straight to the top.

A bit like asking Joshua Bell for violin coaching. There ain't nuffin' like knowing nothing and nobody.

I've now learned what I would look for in a coach if I was looking for one…if you get my drift.

Here are a few attributes that I think are important.

#1 **They need to be your number one cheerleader.**

There are going to be so many times when you are full of self doubt and you need to have someone who is capable of seeing your brilliance even when it seems that no one else, especially yourself, can.

I love this quote by Benjamin Disraeli:

'The greatest good you can do for another is not just to share your riches, but to reveal to him his own.'

You need a coach who is wise and intuitive but who can also recognize and encourage *your* wisdom and intuition.

#2 You need to feel *safe* with them.

This, of course, is about knowing that they are totally professional and will respect your need for confidentiality as a client.

But, almost more importantly, knowing that you can say what is in your heart without any risk of being judged, ridiculed, put down, told off or painfully ignored.

I reckon we all got enough of that for free when we were children without having to pay for it as adults!!

#3 They are unattached to your limiting beliefs and challenge you to change them.

This is where a coach, as opposed to a kind uncle, parent or sibling, is so helpful. Although they are compassionate and empathetic, a good coach doesn't get sucked into your 'story'.

On the contrary. They invite you to look at where you might be holding yourself back by recognizing and challenging your limiting beliefs and letting you see them from the point of view of a lovingly detached observer.

If you are trying to grow and make changes, it is vital to have someone who thinks outside your box. They can help you to expand that box and to think differently and bigger than you ever have before.

So they challenge you and urge you onwards to bigger and better things.

And if they can act as a role model in terms of success and happiness, so much the better.

#4 **Humor and fun.**

This cannot be underestimated. This whole process can be so difficult and downright sad at times and to have someone sympathetic, but who can also inject a little lightheartedness into the mix is a godsend. It also helps if they get your sense of humor too. Nothing like making your coach crack up with laughter to make you feel good about yourself.

#5 **Professionality.**

On the other hand, having someone who is reliable and professional is a must too. After all this is a professional relationship. You're not just chatting to a friend. You need someone who will show up and then follow through, all within reasonable bounds.

Of course, this is a two way street. If we have a coaching call at 8pm then I will do my utmost to be there bang on time, expecting the same from my coach. (Skype problems permitting.)

This is certainly a tappable issue! Often lack of punctuality or following up with promised information shows resistance at some deeper level. (I can hear you thinking: 'Now she wants my coach to learn EFT!!'...I can think of worse things!)

I've been especially lucky with my Life Coach because as well as being extremely professional himself he has also given me professional opportunities. I've played concerts at his workshops and he puts links to my music and videos in his monthly newsletter, *Success Beyond Belief*, thereby sending a message of his confidence in me which has been so valuable for my own self-esteem.

There is one last attribute that I think separates a *good* coach from a *great* coach.

Drum roll here…this is **the ability to** *let you go*.

#6 They are there when you need them and let you 'fly solo' when you need that.

I remember one very emotional session when I came, reluctantly, to the conclusion, that it was important for me to be big and brave and independent and try doing without coaching sessions for a while.

Instead of trying to convince me that I 'needed' a coach in order to make the most of myself, Brad said: 'Well, *there comes a time when you have to take the training wheels off your bike and go it alone.*'

He also made it clear to me that he was there for me if I wanted but that I could also handle life on my own.

By giving me permission to continue or not, I was able to stop 'shoulding' on myself and make clear decisions.

We laughed at the thought of me sending an email the very next day with a request for another session…(which I didn't. Who do you think I am?!... it was at least a week later…)

I have also had a couple of other coaches for specific areas during these years. After all, there are so many ways and so many people out there. Don't let the fear of your coach's fragile ego get in the way of your progress!

Finding a coach.

You may be wondering how to go about finding a fabulous coach of your own!

A lot may be instinctive. Consider the following questions:

Do you like their style when you listen to them in interviews or see them on videos or read what they have written?

Do you like and feel inspired by the information they are sharing?

Do you like how they speak about people? Are they at all judgmental?

Will they let you have just one session up front (to see how you work together) or do they insist on a 'package' right from the get go?

Can you afford their services? Do you feel comfortable paying what they ask? Do they insist on a certain frequency of sessions and could that be negotiable?

Good luck on your coaching journey. And remember the old saying:

'When the student is ready, the teacher will appear.'

You're probably much more ready than you think…

5.3 I'd love to stay in touch!

If you have made it this far with me, I thank you from the bottom of my heart.

This book, like Alice's 'Drink me!' bottle, was saying 'Write me!' and things fell into place to aid and abet the telling of this story.

If this helps even just one person to find the courage and the means to follow their dreams and share their gifts and talents with the world, then, for me that really is the icing on the cake and the bubbles in the champagne!

If even just one thing here has helped you to move into the career and life that you love, would you help me to SPREAD THE WORD?

Please share your thoughts, comments and questions through social media (you can find my links in the 'About the Author' section towards the end of the book).

Please let your friends, colleagues and acquaintances know about the book.

Recommend the book to your book club.

I LOVE questions and would love to find out about your journey too.

You can contact me at my website www.jennyclift.com and join 'The Music Insiders' community there for articles, courses, coaching with me, free resources and more!'

Don't miss all the free stuff that has been dotted throughout the book!

> Visit this link:
>
> *www.jennyclift.com/freebonuses*

I wish you so much happiness, fun and success!

Jenny

P.S.

As an independent, self-publishing author, reviews are extremely important, if not to say vital. If you have enjoyed this book I would be extremely grateful if you could post a positive review on Amazon thus helping me to share it with as many people as possible.

To leave a review, go to Amazon.com, search for Jenny Clift - The Music Inside, click on it and then on 'Write a review'.

Notes

Notes

Notes

Notes

Acknowledgements

- Thank you to my family for supporting me and helping me in all my endeavors. You are always here for me and are so vital to my well-being. My husband Alfonso, and my daughters, Elisa, Emma and Silvia. My parents, my sisters Pam and Lucy and their families. And to my wonderful in-laws; Alfonso's parents and siblings, who welcomed me into their family without pressure!
- Thank you to all the violin teachers I have had over the years. Each one has given me something special and has left their mark on my playing and on my life. Especially to Sally Brundan, Dona Lee Croft, Paolo Vieira, Anna Baget and Clayton Haslop (my teacher by Skype!).
- Thank you too to my teachers at school who taught me how to write and spell and to (almost always) avoid splitting infinitives!
- A big thank you to all my musical friends, partners and colleagues over the years. I have laughed and played and learnt and tuned up alongside you and you have shaped my life and career. Especially to Thea, Blanca, Marleen, Carlos, Silvia, Virginia, Marta, Carmen and Beatrix.
- A huge thank you to the guitarist Cy Williams, my partner in the 'Laurus Freestyle Duo', for being so great to make music with, and for giving me permission to offer our music here.
- Many thanks to Gary Craig, the founder of EFT and owner of its official source *http://www.emofree.com/* for his permission to use the material here. I would like to emphasize that the version I give here is my own and does not necessarily reflect the views of EFT or Gary Craig.
- Thank you to all the friends I have met through EFT. I discovered that you don't have to be weird to be into this kind of thing – just open-minded and big-hearted. Especially to Tracy, Jeanette, Chrissy, Bairbre, Elaine,

Deaconu, Melanie, Sharon, Bill, Tom, Erik, and the members of the BY Facebook groups.
- A thank you too to Lars Rasmusenn and members of the Lastermind group; Georgie, Brett, Debbie and Ron.
- With the help of Chandler Bolt's Self-Publishing School I have been able to get this book down on paper and out into the world in record time. Thank you to my SPS coach, Megan Jamison, who encouraged me to go with my preferred title and who has advised me throughout the process.
- Through the SPS I have met many fantastic people and their books. Especially Claudia Svartefoss (the author of the Amazon bestseller 'Positively Perfect'…and she really walks her talk, creating my wonderful new website, helping to keep me accountable and advising me on so many things), Thor Inge Svartefoss and the members of the SPS and the Positively Perfect Facebook groups. Thanks too to Kylie Ansett who helped me immensely with my subtitle and the look of the front cover.
- My editors Chrissy Disendorff and Elaine MacDonald have polished the book and been so wonderful with their suggestions and feedback.
- My beautiful cover was designed by Heidi Sutherlin who patiently led me to discovering how I wanted it to look and then created it.
- In the book I mention many writers and online course-builders who have shared their incredible wisdom and from whom I have benefited enormously in the area of personal growth. (See Part 5, chapter 1 for a Further Resources link.)
- I say it a lot, and will say it again; thank you to Brad Yates, my amazing EFT Life Coach.

About the Author

Jenny Clift is a professional freelance violinist who currently lives in Madrid, Spain, and works (plays!) with several different symphony orchestras and with her violin and guitar duo (the 'Laurus Freestyle Duo'), as well as making CDs, recordings, Youtube videos and Online courses.

She is married to a wonderful man and has three awesome daughters.

'The Music Inside' is her first book.

Author Website: www.jennyclift.com
Musician Website: www.jenniferclift.com
Facebook: Jenny Clift Author
Twitter: @JennyClift1
LinkedIn: Jennifer Clift

Printed in Great Britain
by Amazon